AN AUTHENTIC EXPERIENCE

Creating an Inviting Culture with Biblical Integrity.

COREY TRIMBLE

This book is dedicated to my wife, Alicia, because she has always encouraged me and pushed me to be more, to my daughters, Aia and Vy, for always leaving me positive messages on my office whiteboard and being the light even at young ages, and to my Savior Jesus Christ for redeeming such a broken vessel.

CONTENTS

PREFACE

I hope this is a book that works on a couple of different levels. First, I hope that virtually all Christians can read the first third of this book and use the principles and stories to connect with non-Christians in their community and lead them into a relationship with Jesus Christ. Secondly, I hope that pastors and church leaders can not only learn to be evangelists as well but also learn to develop an environment in the local church that models the attitudes and ideas mentioned in this book, and most fundamentally, in the Good Book. I hope that, by reading this book, both lay leaders and vocational ministers can take a humble step back into the simplicity of the gospel message. There, they will find simple advice that can put them and their church on a healthy trajectory. The truth is, the church—both the individuals that make up the church and the church as an organization—is struggling. We have not flourished in the last decade and have even declined at an alarming rate. We need help. We need to wake up.

At the core of everything I hope to cover in this book is the tension of maintaining biblical integrity and creating a culture that is welcoming to all people regardless of where they are in life and faith. If we can manage that tension, we can create a great personal, church, and discipleship culture. The lack of managing the tension between cultivating integrity and welcoming everybody may be the single biggest problem that has crippled the church in the last thirty to forty years. We have gone to extremes, either legalistic or liberal, and we are starting to look shockingly like the Pharisees and Sadducees that our Savior pushed against because of their arrogance and lack of biblical integrity.

I promise I am not a pessimist or anti-church. I am actually quite the opposite when it comes to the Body of Christ. I agree with my fellow church leaders who have said that the local church is the hope of the city. I firmly believe that the church is God's instrument to change the hearts of people. Yet I am saddened at how far the majority of churches in the United States have drifted from the simple yet profoundly powerful teachings of the Bible.

I became a Christian in late 2002. Since that time nearly eighteen years ago, I have noticed an almost desperate attempt in the church to somehow achieve relevance and acceptance from a world that Jesus clearly told us would never fully accept us. We have tried gimmicks and giveaways. We've tried using secular music and changing the words a little. We've tried all kinds of other lame ways to grow. Now we are going to even more radical extremes by sacrificing biblical and theological integrity through accepting cultural norms as normative in the church. Oddly enough, a constant bend to the world has not made the church grow but is slowly killing it.

In 2015, a medium-sized church about thirty minutes from our church announced that they were becoming a gay-affirming church. The announcement of a church in the Bible Belt accepting gay clergy and performing gay marriages made national news, and for about three months the progressive pastor was a national hero outside of the mainstream evangelical movement. Yet, over the next couple of years, the church shrank rapidly. It also started to adopt a Unitarian model which allowed it to begin accepting all faiths as valid. The decline accelerated that much more.

The reason I bring this up is that this story is not unique. I have been all over the country and have seen dozens of churches that thought going with the tide of culture would make the church grow in relevance and number. Ironically, virtually every church that has taken that route is in rapid decline. That is not to say all of them are. I have an old friend who is a gay-affirming pastor, and his church is one of the fastest growing in the country at this time. But, as we will see in this book, numerical growth can be deceiving. If the Bible is true, and "God will not be mocked," the true church will not grow if the Word's integrity is tampered with.

So let me get back to the point of this preface. We are in a pivotal time in the narrative of the American church. If we do not work diligently to hold onto biblical truth while also inviting all kinds of people in, we will fail.

What is at stake if we fail to create a personal culture that brings people into disciple-making churches? Christians will no longer be discipled to go out and be the light of their communities. People, communities, neighborhoods, schools, governments, and virtually everyone will suffer in the long run. We need to get to work.

PART 1
PERSONAL CULTURE?

The goal for this section is going to be remarkably simple in theory, but it may be difficult in practice. Part 1 will focus on our own personal culture. The goal is to become the kind of person who creates relationships with nonbelievers and eventually is an aid in leading them to Christ—but without sacrificing our biblical integrity or our welcoming demeanor. This may sound fairly simple, but we are obviously missing the mark since modern Christianity is suffering and declining in an alarming way.

I hope this section is both clear and encouraging. I also hope that it challenges you to get out of your comfort zone and look at other people and yourself a little differently. I pray that you reject the lie that we cannot be both inviting to all and biblically sound at the same time. So I hope to explore not only what we should do but how we can accomplish it. Just a heads up: most of the principles and ideas in this section will seem exceptionally simple in theory but can be quite difficult and draining to put into practice.

Let me also mention this as we begin: All the strategy in the world will not compensate for a lack of prayer and fasting. There must be an anointing of God on the leader and even on the everyday Christian if a church is to create an inviting culture with biblical integrity. If what is covered in this book, or any book outside of the Bible that we read, is not first blanketed with prayer, fasting, and meditation on God and his will, everything we try to accomplish will eventually fall flat.

I also want to clarify that I have not figured it all out, nor has the church I lead. Many of these principles and ideas are put into effect in our church and in our personal lives. Yet my team and I have not mastered the task of discipling everyone we hope to, though we are working diligently to do the best we can with God's grace and guidance. I have a slight fear that in speaking through the lens of what God has done here at The Experience Community, I may come off as self-centered in this book, and that is not how I want to come off. I try to encourage from what I've experienced God do, so that's why I use so many personal stories and stories from people on my team and in my church.

That being said, I encourage you to spend some deep time in prayer before you tackle this book and anything suggested in it.

CHAPTER 1
THE DILEMMA

Since authenticity is going to be a huge focus of this book, I want to start off by being exceptionally honest: I cannot stand the way most Christians, especially pastors, talk and communicate with other people. I confess that one of my least favorite groups to be in the middle of is a group of pastors or cultural Christians. Now, I know that sounds like an awful thing to say, especially for a pastor, but this is me being up-front and honest. When I see videos of pastors talking in ways that anyone outside of their microcosm would never relate to, I actually get angry. Maybe because I feel like so many church leaders are terribly out of touch with the world around them. Or maybe the reason I get so agitated is that I feel like many church leaders and Christians in general are insincere. The insider talk and scary resemblance to the marketing and self-absorbedness of the world seem like a legitimate cause for concern. We have become increasingly isolated as we fumble the ball on how to communicate in a way that builds relationships that lead to discipleship.

Because of many Christians' lack of connection to the people that surround us every day in our grocery stores, coffee shops, and gyms, these Christians' insider language starts to become the language of the church as a whole. This way, churches become groups of people that have almost completely lost the ability to connect and converse with people that are different from them—most importantly, with people that don't know Christ.

I think many of us have passed the task of evangelism off to person X. Maybe it is purely subconscious, but many of us don't have the important role of connecting to lost people at the forefront of our minds. Maybe this is because we are terrified of offending people. Maybe it is because we think we are incapable because we are ill-equipped. Or maybe many of us don't think the problem is urgent. Whatever the reason is, we Christians are not creating intentional relationships with lost people as we should be.

As Christians—who are people that claim to follow Jesus—we have forgotten that Jesus was the perfect model of how to converse with people that are not only lost but are vastly different culturally from those that are saved. In our day, many Christians would find the idea of having a normal conversation with an atheist, Buddhist, Muslim, or transgendered woman a huge source of anxiety or just so uncomfortable for them that they would avoid it at all costs. I will boldly say that these anxious, uncomfortable attitudes are not the heart of our Savior!

Christ was amazing not only at having conversations, but at having them with the most marginalized people. My mind goes to John Chapter 4 when Jesus intentionally began a conversation with a woman who was racially and religiously different from him. I also think of John Chapter 8 when Jesus showed mercy to a woman who had been caught in adultery, a sin that was regarded as one of the worst things someone could do in that time. Jesus went out of his way to engage people who were marginalized. Of course, it wasn't just the marginalized. Jesus conversed with and poured his life into aristocrats (Nicodemus), businessmen (Peter and Zacchaeus), and blue-collar workers (James and John) alike. He knew the poor (the bleeding woman in Luke Chapter 8) and the rich (Joseph of Arimathea). Jesus loved and reached out to all kinds of people, and so should we. This is why the first major problem we will be confronting in this book is the lack of authentic relationships being built—relationships which could ultimately point toward a relationship with Jesus.

The other radical swing of that pendulum is to relent on good theology and blend in so much with the culture around us that we compromise the core teachings of our faith. We become a people that are not "peculiar" and set apart (1 Pet. 2:9, KJV), but half-hearted novices of the gospel. We become exactly what Paul warned Timothy about, people that only have ears to hear and live out the easy parts of our faith (2 Tim. 4:3–4).

Let's return to the remarkable ability Jesus had to communicate and relate to all kinds of people. In doing this, Jesus never compromised the mission, vision, and values of the kingdom in which he resides as King. What we see in Jesus is perfect and unrelenting integrity. He loves all, and he loves them so much that he knows that compromising the faith is not what is best for their souls or even for their temporary lives on earth. This is the second great problem that I hope we tackle throughout this book: how not to compromise our faith for the sake of building relationships.

American Christianity has become remarkably biblically illiterate. This might be because many American pastors don't communicate the value of the Word like they should. It could also be because our fear of cultural retaliation is greater than our fear of God. Again, in the spirit of honesty for the sake of this book, I am nauseated by the lack of spine within the American church at the moment.

The church often lands in either of two polar opposites in society. And neither are working. We become too isolated inside our Christian culture, or we compromise our integrity from the pressure of a worldly culture. Either way, we have moved into a very dangerous compromise of integrity. We should not have to choose between holding on to strong biblical ties or winning people to Jesus. The fact is, we cannot do one without the other.

Why are we not making more followers of Jesus? Could our problem be an issue of the environment we create, both in our personal interactions with others and how we communicate the gospel in our churches? How can we introduce the gospel and make authentic followers of Christ without compromising biblical theology? We also need to ask how we can create an environment to connect with people before they become a part of the church and Christian community. Also, how do we create a similar environment for discipling them after they have given their lives to Christ? There are really three stages where we must intentionally create a culture that fosters authentic followers of Christ: before people are willing to come to church, after they start attending the local church, and when they are ready to be sent out to make more disciples of Jesus.

After The Experience Community started to rapidly grow several years ago, I starting getting people from all over the place asking us what the secret was. Is it the building? Is it cool music? Should I dress a certain way or make up a catchier sermon series? Do we need to make all of our walls look like reclaimed wood? The answer to these shallow questions is always a resounding "no." Yet without fail, people would come visit the building and take pictures of our environment so they could somehow replicate the artwork and décor. Or they would ask what our set list was the past weekend.

In looking simply at the superficial, people miss the real reason why their church is dying. The problem is unfortunately much deeper than just the style of church leadership. In the majority of the churches we work with and who ask for our advice, we have discovered there is a *culture* problem. No one wants to hear that they must work more diligently to foster lasting relationships, that their methods of attracting new believers aren't working, or that they have no plan of discipling people once they come to the church. But people, even Christians with the best intentions, naturally want quick fixes that take the least amount of work and resistance. Unfortunately, the kingdom doesn't grow without some hard, spiritual elbow grease.

We have gotten so many calls for help because so many churches are not growing, or even worse, they are getting smaller. Equally as bad, or worse, is that a lot of the churches that had grown over the years had compromised biblical theology in order to "succeed." For them, it wasn't about making authentic followers of Christ and his principles, but about filling the seats, amassing a fan base, or making sure the livelihood of the staff wasn't compromised. Though many of the churches we met with were not growing because of well-masked selfishness, many times the reason churches were not growing wasn't because pastors were self-centered or the congregation didn't want to grow and reach their area. It was simply because they didn't know how to create the environment of evangelism that leads to discipleship.

I remember when I was a student pastor (we called them youth pastors in 2006) and I was taking my students to a district youth rally in a small rural town called Unionville in middle Tennessee. I was quite the hotshot in the denomination I was saved in and had a pretty large group, especially for the size of our church. I was the tattooed, ex-punk, rock-star-turned-youth pastor, and I kind of reveled in that identity. As we got to the rally, we went in for the service with maybe twenty or so other churches from our district and had an energetic worship night with some preaching at the end.

I met some of the other youth ministers, one being the host youth pastor from the Pentecostal church in Unionville that was only a fraction of the size of my home church. Yet, oddly enough, the youth pastor of this smaller church had a huge group of middle- and high-school-aged kids! Not just that; he was a complete nerd! He was going bald, he tucked his t-shirt into his jeans, and he couldn't play sports worth a flip at the after party in the gym following the service. But as I watched this nerdy, uncoordinated student pastor with his kids, God convicted me and taught me a huge lesson that night. This guy was deeply involved in the lives of his students. He embraced his nerdiness, and the kids loved him! The visitors that his students had brought were magnetized to him, and God was using him in an amazing way. I was stunned and humbled that night. This guy wasn't trying to be anything other than what God made him to be, and it was working! I learned a lot of good lessons that night:

1. God can use anyone that is humble and willing.
2. Most people don't care how cool you are; they just want to be loved and valued.
3. Loving people in a biblical way will lead them to Christ. We think we know that, but we don't live it!

We work with several churches in New England, an area of this country that has less church participation and affiliation with Christianity than anywhere else in America, sometimes getting as low as 1 percent church attendance. As we have worked with these churches for the last six years or so, the excuses some of the churches give us for their lack of growth sometimes frustrate me. I love this area very much, but we have even parted ways with several churches because of their lack of desire to do things differently. And though we pick up new churches to support in New England, it can be difficult to find leaders who are humble enough to listen to outside suggestions. We would often hear things like, "Well, this is New England, and it is tough up here." To be fair, these areas are extremely difficult. It can be a very slow burn approach as it requires a lot of relationship building over a long period of time. But didn't the gospel spread in Greece and Asia Minor, and eventually become the official religion of the Roman Empire? I think God can work in any area, but I also understand that growth is relative depending on where one plants a church. Nonetheless, the point remains the same: healthy organisms grow regardless of the location. The biggest problem wasn't the city in which these churches were planted, but the mindset of the individuals leading those congregations.

As I would interact with the pastors of New England churches in restaurants and as we walked around their cities, I would observe their interactions, or lack thereof. I noticed that I would engage with and get to know more people than they did. Not only were many of these church leaders isolated in public, but their lay leaders and congregations also lacked the drive to create conversations that opened up doors for people to become disciples of Jesus. I would often get dumbfounded when we would go to a local coffee shop and whereas I was the one creating conversations with the baristas, the senior pastor wouldn't even introduce himself. How can a church possibly grow without the pastor leading the charge of engaging with the community?

One of the most interesting relationships I created was in Salem, Massachusetts, after I visited the Satanic Temple (that won't be the last thing that makes you uncomfortable in this book). I took three of my team members and the pastor from the church in Salem with me to the temple because I have studied the occult extensively and because I wanted to see the reason for all the uproar about this temple. While in the temple, I got to know the curator. We talked for about thirty minutes about all kinds of things, and of course about how he became a part of the Satanic movement. I told him what I did for a living, which made him laugh out loud. I also told him how confused my accountant would be at the church when she saw the receipt from the Satanic Temple. He didn't drop to his knees in repentance, he didn't accept Christ on the spot, but a connection between us was made.

A couple of months later, I was back in Salem to talk with some board members from the church there and help them do some strategizing. Before our meeting I wanted to get some coffee at my favorite little coffee spot in the area. As I was sipping my drink, my new Satanic friend walked in, instantly saw me, and said, "Hey! The pastor from Tennessee!"

I laughed and said, "Hey! The Satan guy from Salem!"

What happened in that moment was that this confused young man learned that not all Christians scream at gay people on the streets of Salem during Halloween. What he learned is that some of us are not afraid to engage with people vastly different from us. Some of us even laugh with diametrically opposed people. For some reason we have created a narrative in our culture, both Christian and secular, that we cannot be friendly with people we disagree with. I find this not only troubling but antithetical to the teachings of Christ.

It goes almost without saying that the American church has gone through some tumultuous times in the short eleven years that The Experience has existed. So we started to ask ourselves, as others were asking us as well, *What can we contribute to the conversation as to why the church seems to be in such disarray?* Though I don't profess to know all the answers, I have learned through our own tumultuous times that:

- Genuinely loving others, even the most extreme of people, honors God and opens the door for them to have a relationship with him.
- We cannot compromise our biblical integrity for the sake of being accepted. Compromising theology will never lead people into an authentic relationship with Christ. In fact, it will set them up for failure and discouragement.

Though it may take much work and diligence, we believe that with God's grace and guidance any church can become a place that both welcomes the lost and stands strong in biblical integrity.

Again, our dilemma lies in the extremes we tend toward in our current societal state: cultural nonengagement and biblical faithlessness. Unfortunately, the church is rapidly growing irrelevant because we have not engaged a struggling world around us with love and integrity.

Fun fact for you pastors reading this book: the first growth barrier in the life of a church is the 200-person mark that a vast majority of churches in the United States never crest. If one researches church growth barriers, one will discover that the first 200 people are typically a result of the connection the pastor has to their community. If you are reading this and your church is less than 200 people, the problem may simply be you. I am not trying to hurt your feelings, but I am trying to prod you to go out and make connections in your community!

TAKE AN INVENTORY:

1. Do you find it more tempting to isolate yourself from the culture around you or to compromise your biblical convictions in order to fit in with the culture?
2. Can you think of any quick fixes that Christians and church leaders have taken to grow the church but failed in? How did these tactics make you feel?

CHAPTER 2

DEFINING PERSONAL CULTURE (AND OTHER CORE TERMS IN THIS BOOK)

Culture is a term that is used often and can have many different interpretations. We hear corporations talk about their work culture, we hear people from other nations talk about their culture, we talk about culture in relation to music and entertainment, and we even hear this word a lot in Christian circles, especially churches. It is a great thing to talk about culture because culture really encompasses the depths of the human experience. Culture plays a part in who we spend time with, how we work and play, how we live in our homes, and even how we function within our religious circles.

Marketing firms spend millions of dollars a year trying to capture or create a culture in order to sell goods. Businesses spend countless hours and large amounts of money trying to develop an attractive culture that draws the top talent. Artists, musicians, and filmmakers strive to speak to and create culture. Even churches have jumped on the bandwagon of studying and trying to create culture, although most churches seem a little late and reactive to the world's already established culture. So if Apple, Google, Beyoncé, Netflix, and the megachurch on TV are all striving to capitalize on and create culture, why are we as Christian individuals not thinking more about the culture we create?

Before we get into what personal culture is, let's first talk about how we evaluate culture in general. The word *culture* originated in France but is derived from the Latin *colere*, which means to tend to the earth or to cultivate and nurture something in order for it to grow. I know that may seem a little out of left field, but really think about that definition of culture. It is essentially saying that to make something grow and flourish we must tend to and cultivate it. Cultivation takes time, knowledge, and hard work. This lets us know that the creation or changing of culture is going to be a process that will take intentional hard work.

Several organizations have derived "Culture Wheels" that help show what encompasses and makes up culture. NMAC, an organization that helps with the treatment and prevention of HIV amongst minorities in America, has come up with the best model and implementation of a Culture Wheel that I have seen. After talking with one of their directors, I was told that this model is a starting point to create conversations within a given community. According to this Culture Wheel, there are nine tools at our disposal to help us build bridges with virtually any kind of person or people group.

These are nine values that NMAC uses to understand and connect with people groups (we will explain them in detail later):[1]

1. Knowledge and Stories
2. Language
3. Traditions and Rituals

4. Techniques and Skills
5. Tools and Objects
6. The Arts
7. Food and Drink
8. Values
9. Greater Community

Though these nine bridge-building values are used to define "worldly" cultural movements and how we can connect to them, understanding how we function within these can really help the Christian community connect with people around us. Within the context of Christianity, understanding these nine values can help us as we begin the command of the Great Commission found in Matthew 28:19–20. To be able to reach people, we must start to understand how people and cultures are comprised and how they work.

Maybe one of our biggest problems in Christian culture is that we don't intentionally create it. We tend simply to let culture happen to us. But if culture is made up of the collective values of the people, what would happen if Christians, as individuals that make up what the Bible calls a collective "peculiar people," started to take their cultural contribution to the greater body more seriously? If we took the nine values mentioned earlier to heart and asked how we as individuals cultivate and nurture our personal culture, what would happen to the culture of our churches, neighborhoods, coffee shops, and wherever else we as individual followers of Christ may go?

Let's be realistic. I don't think we will ever completely change the culture of the world (because Christ basically tells us this). But we can change the culture within our personal sphere of influence. In other words, we can create a personal culture that affects those that come in contact with us within the greater culture of the world. So let's talk more about cultivating personal culture.

Personal Culture

In this book we will be using the term *personal culture* quite often. This term simply means the attitude and actions that we develop and practice while around both Christians and nonbelievers. The idea is that if businesses and churches work hard to create a culture of relationship and progress, individual Christians should be doing something very similar. Personal culture in the most practical sense is how we engage with the people around us. It is how we communicate our passions and values, how we find out about other people's values and dreams, and how we create lasting relationships over time. Good personal culture involves integrity, honesty, and most importantly, a love for others.

A personal culture comes from a repentant heart that follows Jesus Christ. One way to define repentance is to "change the way one thinks and acts." We often think repenting is simply asking for God's forgiveness, which of course is a huge part of repentance. But the full action of repenting is choosing to go the direction that removes us from sin and darkness. If we are to change our personal culture, we must choose to be a part of Jesus' culture. We must not only turn from sin, but we must adopt the heart of God to follow his direction which includes making disciples that make more disciples.

It is only from a connection with Christ and a desire to follow his commands that we are able to take what we have learned about the Culture Wheel and use it to advance the kingdom of God. Going back to NMAC's Culture Wheel, how can we take these core values of culture and use them to share the gospel with others? Let's briefly define the nine values of the Culture Wheel and see how we can use these bridge-building values in our daily lives.

1. Knowledge and Stories. We all have life experiences that give us a unique ability to connect with people around us. We also have stories to share. One of my favorite ways to connect with people I don't know is asking them to tell me their life story. I mean it kind of jokingly, but I want to hear a paragraph version of how they ended up where they are. Stories are connecting points that are invaluable because they show others that we not only care about their place in the universe but that we also have similar experiences. This is where we need to really listen to others and try to find ways to share similar experiences.

What do we know and what kind of life stories do we have that can be a way to connect with people? Maybe you have the same bachelor's degree, have similar training in electrical work, or studied the same authors. Or maybe you both had fathers that left you in your adolescent years. Try to find the learned and experienced things you have in common with others.

2. Language. I live in a very eclectic part of Tennessee. It is a college town that has rapidly grown and has large populations of Laotians, Arabs, Hispanics, and of course African Americans and Caucasians. In our town, it is pretty common to meet people from Asia, Germany, the Middle East, and other places. When I hear not only accents but the verbiage people use when talking, it opens up a door for conversation and getting to know people.

How do you speak? Is there an accent—Boston or Chicago, New York or Louisiana—that you have in common? Is there a foreign language you both know or certain words only people from your region use? How can you connect with others around how you speak?

3. Traditions and Rituals. This can include traditions in families, holidays, cultural traditions from other regions or religious backgrounds, etc. It is amazing to see people who connect over generational traditions. There is almost an instant community that is created when one realizes that someone else also celebrates Hanukkah, does family celebrations for first haircuts as a child, or some other tradition.

What traditions have you begun and how can you share those experiences and connect with other people who are also formulating these traditions in their families? These may be things as simple as Christmas rituals or how you prepare food for your family on birthdays, but the connection from them can be powerful.

4. Techniques and Skills. Again, this can mean a lot of different things, but most specifically something you do well that someone else might also excel in. Can you connect with someone over woodworking, restoring cars, crafts, or making jewelry? Even your occupations and what you do for a living can be some of the easiest ways to find a connection with someone.

5. Tools and Objects. This is essentially the same as skills, but maybe more specific in how you do your skill. If someone likes cars, how do they work on them? What kind of cars do they prefer? Are there certain methods and instruments used to master their skill? If someone is a guitar player, what kind of amp do they prefer?

6. The Arts. This is one that I shine in and where most people will find the easiest connection to others. This includes the music you listen to, the movies you watch, the artists that captivate you, and the writers that write books you can't put down. What kinds of movies, music, arts, and books do you both like? What is a TV show you both love? How do you find new music? This is such an easy way to connect with virtually anyone! This is why I advocate Christians wearing band t-shirts, using phone cases with their favorite artist on it, or talking about their favorite TV shows. Simple cultural connections can be made by our love of the arts!

7. Food and Drink. The Bible talks many times about the importance of "breaking bread" with one another. Sitting down for coffee or getting lunch with someone can be an amazing connecting point with others. My wife and I love sushi, and that love alone has opened up doors for us to sit with other people and get to know them. We sometimes underestimate the cultural connection with food and drink. There are people who will pay $500 for a small bottle of bourbon, $50 for a fine cigar, $100 for the best sushi, and $75 for a good steak. Even if our tastes aren't this fancy or deep, we can connect with people over dinner or coffee.

8. Values. This one can get a little tricky when communicating with people who are not followers of Jesus because many of our values will not align. Yet even with people of very different values, you can most likely come to an agreement on things like seeking justice, treating people well, showing respect, and agreeing on similar universal truths that permeate almost every culture and people. The trick is to find common ground and start to build from that.

If we will take the time to research other world religions, we will see that we do have some common values with almost all of them. This is not to lead us to some kind of religious pluralism which teaches that all religions are true, but to help us find a way to connect with nonbelievers.

9. Greater Community. I live in Murfreesboro, Tennessee, but I am from St. Louis. When I meet others from St. Louis, I always ask, "What part of the city are you from?" because there is a sense of being a part of a greater community. Pretty much any geographical area has this kind of cultural connection. One isn't from New York City; they're from the Bronx or Manhattan. The connection to greater community is a good way to connect with others. This doesn't have to just be geography; it can be a favorite sports team or maybe a blog that a lot of people are going to for a sense of involvement. To get to a conversation about the greater community, we have to be listening and seizing the opportunities to talk to people.

If we can take some or maybe even all of these nine ways to connect with others via our cultural experiences, we can start to create a personal culture that looks similar to how Jesus interacted with people throughout the Gospels. Also, from knowledge of culture we can create a healthy personal culture that will hopefully create opportunities to disciple other people. The point is to find the door. If we don't intentionally find openings to get to know people, we cannot properly love them and lead them to the source of all love, Jesus Christ.

Disciple and Discipleship

Defining *disciple* and *discipleship* takes a lot of clarity and description because of the extremely wide interpretations of what it means to make a disciple. To make disciples—that is, fully devoted followers of Jesus Christ—is one of the clearest and most direct commands from God's Son, given shortly before he left in body to prepare to send the Holy Spirit on the day of Pentecost. Keep in mind that our discussion of personal culture is meant to help us accomplish the real goal of making more disciples of Jesus.

Christianity uses the word *disciple* virtually all the time. Yet, according to David Kinnaman and Mark Matlock's research in their profoundly important work *Faith for Exiles: 5 Ways for a New Generation to Follow Jesus in Digital Babylon*, it turns out that very few Americans that claim to follow Christ actually know what it really means to be a disciple of Jesus. Though a majority of young Americans—roughly 78 percent of 18- to 29-year-olds—still claim Christianity, I would argue that we as a society have become post-Christian. After all, only 10 percent of this younger generation matches the biblical criteria of what it means to truly be a disciple of Jesus.[2] So in order to move forward, we must paint a clear picture of what a disciple of Jesus really is.

For the sake of this book, we are going to define a disciple of Jesus as someone who wholeheartedly and genuinely follows Jesus, follows the written Word of God despite cultural shifts, and is faithfully involved in a local church. Let me also point out that there are several other strong ways to frame what a disciple is and what disciple-making looks like. For example, Discipleship.org defines a disciple as "someone who is following Jesus, being changed by Jesus, and is committed to the mission of Jesus" (Matt. 4:19). As such, disciple-making includes both evangelism *and* discipleship. Discipleship.org goes on to say,

Unfortunately, in the North American church, discipleship is typically seen as an educational process designed to orient new believers to the biblical and everyday practices of our churches. We try to focus on disciple making, but will sometimes use the expression "relational discipleship" to show that there is more than just education behind Jesus-style disciple making.[3]

This shouldn't be taken to imply that education is not part of the process in becoming a disciple of Jesus. Jesus took three years to educate, demonstrate, and empower his disciples to go and accomplish the mission he had for them. The point is that disciple-making is more than adapting a body of teaching to a particular church model. It involves transmitting the Bible's teaching through the relational model which Jesus set forth for all believers.

Many churches are doing a good job acclimating people to their churches, but not doing so well discipling them in a deep relationship with Jesus. Discipleship.org and Exponential.net partnered together in some pretty serious research on how effective and present disciple-making is in the American church, and the results were pretty rough. They concluded that less than 5 percent of churches in the United States are making true disciples of Jesus.[4] Now I know it is easy to blame the church, but aren't all believers the makeup of the church? In other words, we are all responsible.

Authenticity

The word *authentic* is a buzzword in both corporate America and church circles. It would be a more helpful word if more people practiced it and we had a clearer understanding of it. As it stands, we have become a generation that has mastered the art of an alternate reality. Our biggest celebrities are "reality" TV stars. Our marketing campaigns from virtually every market are all about trying to sell us on what is supposedly real and genuine. If I were to take Facebook or Instagram as authentic portraits of people's lives, I would be led to believe that everyone is always on vacation and they laugh out loud when they eat bagels while reading their Bibles. In other words, we aren't always authentic.

Our definition for authenticity will simply be when a person lives honestly and in accordance with how they feel about a particular idea or situation. This term is so vitally important to the DNA of this book and the ideas within it because without genuine conversations, honest feelings, and just being who God made us to be, none of the practices or ideas in this book will work. In my humble opinion, the lack of authenticity and integrity in the church—and by church,

I mean all of us that claim to be followers of Jesus—has been one of the greatest factors of its decline over the last several decades.

TAKE AN INVENTORY:

1. What are two or three obstacles that have kept you from building strong connections with nonbelievers?
2. What are two or three bridge-building points of connection you read about in this chapter which give you a realistic picture of how you can connect with nonbelievers?

CHAPTER 3

DO I LOVE PEOPLE? HONESTLY?

*"The Experience was the first genuine encounter I ever had
with the Holy Spirit. It was so evident the first time I came
into the building, even before service began. The people in the
room seemed, for lack of a better word, raw. There were no false
pretenses of perfection like I had experienced so many times before
in so many churches."*

—Sara Matheny, former Mormon and Founder of Emerge
Special Needs Ministry

I remember when I got saved in August of 2002; I instantly
fell head over heels for Jesus. I know that sounds goofy,
but I did. I was reading the Bible nonstop, I was at church
every time the doors were open, and I was praying four or five
times a day. But, as much as I loved God and a couple of key
people in my life, overall I could not stand humanity. I would
walk through the mall or go to the university I was about
to graduate from and just loathe people. I had been hurt by
family. I had seen the darkest corners of society when I was
deep in my sinful nature. Even my newfound relationship
with God (because I was immature in my faith) made me
look at people that hadn't found what I had with contempt
and judgment. I clearly remember the day it hit me that I was

blatantly ignoring the second most important teaching of Jesus: to love my neighbor (Mark 12:31).

The church I came to know Christ in had a very small prayer room off the main hallway. At one point, I went into that prayer room, moved over a couple of fake plants, and lay on the floor near the corner asking God to put a love in my heart for people. Loving people is very unnatural for many of us; therefore, we must tap into the supernatural power of God to put that love in us. I recall lying there, begging God to break down the walls of my very hardened heart toward people. I wanted not only to honor God but also to have the ability to go out and show people the love he had shown me. God was faithful to my request, and immediately my eyes were open to how wonderful and broken people can be. I became, and still very much am, an extremely empathetic person. Though I can get frustrated with people and need my space at times, I can honestly say I love people. Much to my wife's chagrin, I have become the guy on the airplane that always asks the person next to me where they are from and how the book is that they're reading. Don't judge me too harshly though, I give them their space sometime after takeoff.

We talk a lot in Christian circles about loving people, but do we really live that out? I would walk through the halls of my college or the mall and silently judge the scantily clad young woman or make derogatory remarks about the gay couple, the whole time claiming to be a follower of Christ. I wasn't a lover of people; I was actually a loather of them. Even if many pastors or Christians have never sunk to the depths of loathing others, many of us love people only conditionally and if we can share common interests or life experiences. Jesus said even the nonbelievers can pull that off! Often times we aren't interested in diverse community. Instead, we love lifestyle enclaves that isolate us from every person different from ourselves.

I remember when I first came across the term *lifestyle enclave.* I was studying a commentary for Ecclesiastes and the commentator used this term. It simply means that we create environments that are filled with people and ideologies that we are comfortable with. In a very serious way, the church is guilty of building such environments to the exclusion of others. When we invite politicians into our pulpits, demonize certain demographics of nonbelievers, and make snide remarks about people that are different from us, we create lifestyle enclaves. This is not what the church is called to be. Yes, we should have a common overarching theology, but within that biblical framework, we should have all kinds of people in different stages of their spiritual walk. For clarity, I am not proposing universalism (everybody gets saved in the end) or turning a blind eye to evil, but I am strongly urging that we create cultures that let people on all levels of their journey toward Jesus come and find solace with other brothers and sisters.

Let's be honest. I am not sure that many of us even know what the biblical definition of *love* is. We love and pray for our government when our party of preference is in office but tend to spew venom when we disagree with who got elected. We love the unborn and fight for their rights while often hating the doctors who perform abortions. We can say very un-Christlike things, such as, "I will respect her when she respects me!" We even have variations within the "family" of God, causing divisions over minor issues while completely neglecting the heresy and darkness in our own hearts. We can throw the word *love* around so carelessly and yet neglect the true teachings on it that came straight from the mouth of Christ. Direct commands to pray for those that persecute us and love our enemies go ignored, even by the most popular and influential Christians. If we are to move people into an authentic relationship with God and other brothers and sisters in Christ, we must first admit that many of us don't love in the proper sense of the word.

Of course, the Word helps us understand love. 1 Corinthians Chapter 13 shows us the actions of love. John 3:16 tells us that love is sacrificial. 1 John 4:8 tells us that we are incapable of true love without God because "God is love." And though there is no short, simple definition of love, the study of the Bible gives us many examples and actions that make up someone that truly loves.

Maybe I am being too harsh and critical. Many people do love others, but simply don't know how to practically live out that love in a way that not only shows others the heart of God but connects them to him. Of course, first and foremost we must go to the Scripture to learn not only how to love others but *why* we should love others. We know from Scripture that we are commanded to love and are able to do so because God has first loved us (1 John 4:19). Furthermore, God has given us the Holy Spirit, who empowers us to be able to love those around us. We learn from the Bible that love comes with discipline. Love can be difficult and full of letdowns and hurt, but we are to keep pursuing love because eternity is at stake. God is the perfect essence of love, and God within us should manifest in us loving others well. The Word makes it clear that love is paramount in the life of a true disciple of Jesus, and true disciples make more true disciples.

Love has always been the catalyst for making diligent followers of Christ. Back in the second year our church existed, a young lady started coming who had no Christian background at all. Kristen was a college kid that came in one Sunday night when we still did Sunday night services. I remember she actually slept during the service the first couple of times she came, but she kept coming and she eventually made it through my sermons. I instantly took a liking to Kristen. She was weird and goofy and she would laugh at times when it really wasn't appropriate, but that's what everyone liked about her. The other thing about Kristen is that she invited everyone to church! She would go out, love people, and then quickly invite them to our small church on the square.

One of those people was a couch-surfing, twenty-something homeless dropout named Patrick. Not only was Patrick homeless, but I found out months later that he was estranged from his wife. But, just like Kristen, Patrick jumped in and became very devoted to the church. He got baptized, started serving with our kids, and became a pivotal part of our volunteer team. In 2011, I took Patrick and some other volunteers to a *Catalyst* conference in Atlanta. While we were there, Patrick heard from God that it was time to fix his marriage. By the following year, I did the couple's vow renewal. Long story short, Patrick eventually became the children's pastor at our church and moved up into a team leadership position over all family ministries. Currently Patrick has several hundred volunteers and over 1,400 children just in his children's department.

A couple of years back, Patrick started discipling a young woman named Sara that had come out of Mormonism and into our church. Sara was working on her master's degree and was starting to serve with kids in our church. Sara's heart was really for kids with special needs, and in 2018 she soft-launched a ministry in our church called Emerge that focuses primarily on kids with special needs. As of today, there are over sixty families that come to our church just because of Emerge. They are families that couldn't attend church before because no one in our county did anything like what we were doing. Think about that: sixty families from just one person's ministry. That is almost twice the size of the average church in the United States. Sara's ministry is now starting to be taught in other churches and even other countries where we do pastoral training.

The point of this story is this: showing love to one quirky college girl that most people would just overlook turned into a homeless twenty-something getting saved and becoming a great leader of families. That homeless twenty-something then led a young former Mormon to start a ministry that has given sixty-plus families in our city alone the opportunity to hear the gospel. The simple love of others and the willingness to share the light of God with them literally transforms more people than we could ever imagine.

If you find yourself reading this and asking if you truly love people, regardless of differences and discomforts, I suggest you find your version of the prayer room with the fake plants and ask God to change your heart. But know that choosing to create a personal culture that longs to love and connect people to Jesus is a messy and sometimes painful road that demands much of us. So often in my ministry over the last eleven years or so, the people that have hurt me the most were the ones I sank the most time, money, energy, and love into. Of course, we have seen some tremendous victories and miracles as well, but the scars of the loved ones gone rogue are still present. Sometimes these scars still cause us apprehension to go too deep with people. Even still, "We love because [God] first loved us" (1 John 4:19).

TAKE AN INVENTORY:

1. What are some ways that love is messier and harder than just "niceness"?
2. "Love" isn't always the first word that nonbelievers think of when they hear the word *Christian*. What are two or three changes you (and your church) could make that would help nonbelievers equate Christians with love?
3. Have you really sought the Lord in prayer about loving others?

CHAPTER 4

HOW DO I START HAVING INTENTIONAL CONVERSATIONS?

I am an opportunist at heart. One of my greatest fears is missing opportunities; it is just the way I am wired. Couple that mindset with a deep love for people and hearing stories, and it makes for me being a pretty good people person (if I do say so myself). I know that not everyone is geared to talk to everyone all the time, but as Christians, we have to learn to be aware and seize every opportunity God gives us to build relationships with people, especially nonbelievers.

Of course, Jesus gives us the perfect example in the story of the woman at the well in John Chapter 4. The interaction Jesus had with a Samaritan woman contains so many practical lessons for how we as followers of Jesus should communicate with nonbelievers and introduce the idea of following him. It is also a story that (ironically enough) flies in the face of how most Christians engage, or neglect to engage, the world around them.

Most people reading this book are probably extremely familiar with the story, but maybe there are some subtle points that many of us have missed. Important points like, Jesus was breaking a huge cultural and religious rule that men didn't speak to women in public areas like he did. The conversation

Jesus had with a woman from Samaria was about the equivalent of a pastor talking to a transgendered man in the middle of a grocery store. How many of us can have a normal conversation in the middle of such an extremely different environment from what we are accustomed to?

Speaking of public areas, Jesus positioned himself to be in a place to meet new people. And, as they talked, Jesus didn't instantly share who he was, but started the conversation about drinking from the well. He then, in the most beautiful way, gently introduced the gospel by using a simple analogy about water and the temporal things of this life. He also concluded with direct clarity, stating exactly who he was. Jesus didn't argue politics. He didn't use words she wouldn't understand. He didn't isolate himself from the problem. He created a conversation opportunity and a woman was forever changed as a result. Basically, John 4:1–26 is a condensed formula for how to engage the lost and lead them to Christ.

When speaking to the very dysfunctional church in Corinth, Paul said that, in order to bring more people to a saving knowledge of Jesus, he had to become "all things to all people" (1 Cor. 9:22). This does not mean that Paul compromised the truth and gospel of Jesus because the culture around him didn't always agree. Rather, it means that Paul adapted his methodology in order to present his theology to a group of people that had different life experiences and views than he did. Theology never changes, because God never changes, but the methodology of how we present the gospel has progressed and changed, and it always should, depending on the needs of the present generation.

One of the best examples of this is from Acts Chapter 17 when Paul references philosophy to the Greeks in Athens. We see from this encounter that we are to not be completely ignorant when it comes to the "philosophies" of the world. I am not advocating that we immerse ourselves in things that are contradictory to our beliefs. But we should be able to talk movies, music, and the arts with the people around us in order to build bridges and find commonality. We as Christians are extremely handicapped if we cannot have normal conversations about things that people are interested in.

We also need not show our surprise at behaviors we don't approve of. I am not saying that we accept sinful behavior, but we cannot expect someone who doesn't have a relationship with Jesus to act like, well, Jesus. I remember several years ago we had our oldest daughter's class over at the end of the school year, and a woman from our church happened to be at our house as well. As the lady from our church and a mom from my daughter's class got to talking with me, it came out that the student's mom was in a throuple: a relationship with three adults. Having come from the past my wife and I do, and hearing and seeing what I have in ministry, nothing really shocks us anymore. But the churchgoer in this conversation with us couldn't have had a more shocked look on her face. Now, I get it; it's not every day that a conversation like this happens, but if we are going to build bridges, we must be able to control our shock, and even repulsion at times, for the sake of getting to know people that are not Christians.

About ten years ago, I was asked to speak at a big church in Michigan. The first night that I was scheduled to speak, one of the pastors of the church picked up me and my wife from the airport. He asked what we wanted to do in the few hours we had before the service that night. We decided to go by the Starbucks close to the church and get some coffee and just chill out before I was scheduled to speak. I wanted to get to know the team there at the church a little bit and learn more about the town I was speaking in.

As we were ordering our coffee, I watched the college pastor text on his phone as he ordered his drink, a pretty common thing to do for the usual customer, but I quickly noticed a missed opportunity to connect with the girl taking our drink orders. The pastor rolled to the end of the counter to wait for his drink, still texting away and not paying attention to the environment around him. I on the other hand quickly said hello to the barista by her name (it was on her name tag) and asked her where she was from and how she ended up in Auburn Hills. I remember I was wearing a Cure shirt (the greatest band ever). She told me she was from Detroit and she had gotten a small scholarship to go to Oakland College, a good-sized state school in that area. I asked what her major was, and she told me English Literature. Oddly enough, this was the same undergraduate degree I got at MTSU in Murfreesboro, Tennessee. I asked what she hoped to do with her degree, and she didn't know.

Then she asked the question that led to something extremely important. She simply asked, "What do you do for a living?" Then I had a very natural opportunity to tell her about the event I was speaking at and how I became a Christian during my junior year in college. She told me she was raised in a Christian home, but had stopped going years ago, like many people her age. I said, "Why don't you come out and hear me teach tonight?" and without batting an eye, she emphatically said that sounded really cool. Though I am obviously not Jesus and Starbucks is not exactly a well, one can see the parallel in the two stories. We need to be looking for the moment to create a conversation and introduce the gospel.

That night when I was about to go out and speak, the college pastor did a brief introduction and told the congregation about how the conversation I had at Starbucks earlier that day had gone. He told the crowd that I talk to people and find common ground with them. I was floored when the congregation applauded my simple conversation. I was further in awe as people flooded me with compliments and praise for having a conversation in a coffee shop. Wow. That small interaction was truly groundbreaking and paradigm shifting for what I then realized was an extremely isolated and unhealthy culture at that particular church. I'm not telling this story to bash that church or to lift myself up, but to point out that creating an environment and culture of loving and relating to people can easily be overlooked—not necessarily from a place of lacking in love for others, but simply from being ignorant on how to practically do it in a real-world setting.

The opportunity to connect and build relationships is around us virtually all the time; the problem is that we are often distracted and not very opportunistic in how we see others. If the opportunities are truly around us all the time, why aren't we seeing and seizing them?

One of the ways that I try to create opportunities is to have a circuit of places I visit. That means that I frequent the same places over and over. In doing this, I get to know the bagger at Kroger, the barista at Starbucks, the sweaty guy on the treadmill next to me, and the waitress at the Thai restaurant with the killer pho. When I engage these people, I make sure that I am present, not on my phone, not talking to whomever I may be with, but focused on them for the brief interaction time that we may have. I get to know people in a natural way. We talk about movies, music, kids, future plans, or just whatever may come up. By being consistent and engaged in other people's lives, we create a culture of relationship that we can take wherever we go. I can't tell you how many people have started attending The Experience because I personally met them in a Starbucks or at the gym.

One of these relationships that I was fortunate to foster was with a barista that had grown up in the church but had strayed far from Jesus. How we met will serve as a launching pad for another important component of creating a culture of discipleship. I remember pulling up to the drive-thru window after lunch to get my grande iced coffee with one Sweet'N Low and light cream when I noticed the barista was wearing a black-and–white, chevron-patterned button-down shirt. Without giving it a ton of thought, I said, "Wow, your shirt reminds me of how much I love *Twin Peaks*." The barista almost dropped my coffee as he told me that was his favorite show of all time and how he hated that more people aren't able to talk about it. We sat there for maybe five minutes discussing all of the theories of the show and expressed our excitement about the long awaited third season after twenty-five years.

Long story short (but we will revisit it later), as this barista and I became friends, we started to hang out outside of the Starbucks. I learned about his abusive childhood, his abusive marriage to his husband, and how his lack of healthy relationship with his father sent him into looking for sexual affirmation from other men. I recall us driving around one night after seeing a movie at the local theater and him telling me about how often his husband hits him and calls him names. Though this particular barista has not yet come to our church, he now has someone in his life to talk to when times are hard. In fact, when his father recently died, I was the only person he told besides his boss at work. Isn't it crazy that when we look for opportunities to connect with people, we become the temporary light that may just lead them to the Source of light? The apostle Paul told us that we are not responsible for the results, but we must plant and water the seed in hopes that something happens (1 Cor. 3:7).

I challenge you to be more present. Intentionally visit the same places, get to know the people in your world, put down the phone, ask questions, and pray for God to open up opportunities for you to share your faith. It is impossible to get to know people when we are too distracted and self-consumed to really see them or acknowledge that they are living life as well. If we want to start the journey of communicating better with people about our faith, perhaps the best place lies in first identifying our audience. I often encourage our congregation to focus on "their world," or their "microcosm."

Though foreign missions are great, my implication in this statement is much more local. When talking about "our world," I am referring to our individual microcosms, i.e., the grocery store we go to weekly, the coffee shops we meet clients at, the gym we need to go to more often, our workplace, our neighborhood, and so on. The point is not to think about geographical space, but the sphere of influence we have on a day-to-day basis in the world in which we function the most often. This is the "world" in which you and I will have the most influence.

When it comes to changing the atmosphere of how people perceive Christ and the Christian faith, I think of Nehemiah. Nehemiah was the man put in charge of rebuilding the walls of Jerusalem after the city was destroyed. It is *how* they rebuilt the wall that applies so well to what we're discussing in this book. No one tried to rebuild the entire wall; rather, each person took his own section to rebuild. In essence, if the atmosphere in our world is going to change, we must take our section of the wall, our "world," and start building a better foundation in order to protect the reputation of our faith and the perception of Christ with the people we have influence over.

The church must also empower and encourage their congregation to be relational and evangelistic in a very natural and organic way. This means that ministry opportunities must be available for people to watch others create relationships so they can become more confident to reach out themselves. One way that our church does this is through our Bar Ministry. Every Friday night, we send a team of people to go serve our city by handing out free hot dogs outside of the bars around our downtown square. Our goal is always to introduce Christ to people that don't know him, and in this case, we do that by giving out some food, water, and coffee to people that leave the bar to go home. Through our interactions, we have also been able to help make sure people get home safely. Our means to opening up conversation is our consistent presence on the square. We rarely if ever have to start the conversation about Jesus. Once people see that we care and want the best for them, they usually want to know why.

Over the last nine years, I have seen dozens of baristas come to know the Lord simply because we first started talking as I was waiting for my iced coffee. Of course, it's not just about coffee shops, but you get the point. If we can slowly build trust over time with the people we see in our corner of the world, one day the conversation will get deeper, even to the point of God and salvation.

I recall one time I was in the line at Starbucks and, just like I would do every day, I asked the barista how her day was going. She started to tear up and asked if I had a couple of minutes to talk. I was actually in quite a hurry, but in that moment, I was reminded of another huge lesson of the faith: though I was in a hurry, talking with someone—especially a nonbeliever—was the highest priority level possible. So she took a fifteen-minute break, came and sat down with me, and we went deep into her family and relationship struggles. I am not sure of the state of the young lady's soul to this day, but I know that I had the chance to listen to her troubles, pray for her, and allow her to at least have some relief in that moment.

It was not my job to save her; it was my job to be available and plant a seed of hope and truth in her heart.

The point is that we have to foster a culture that loves people and wants to get to know them. This will almost always naturally lead to talking about Jesus and inviting people to come and be a part of the church community. If we don't connect with people on a personal level, it makes it virtually impossible to make them followers of Jesus Christ. In America, getting to a point where we can naturally breach the conversation of faith can be a slow burn that takes much care to accomplish.

Here is a simplified list of how I create a personal culture that may lead to a discipleship relationship:

1. I frequent the same places. I go to the same coffee shops for long periods of time, I eat at the same five restaurants, I shop at the same Kroger. In doing this, I see the same people at the checkout lane or serving my food. I get to know them, ask their names, talk about music and movies, ask about school or work. We're talking normal conversation. In doing this, I am cognizant of not being a weirdo. I just act like a nice person. If a local pastor has a smaller congregation or has a new church plant, this is how they grow a church to 200 people. If the leaders of churches are not conversational and relatable, the church likely won't be either.

2. I don't speak "Christianese." (This is a made-up language that only Christians speak.) When I engage in conversation, I talk like a normal person. I consciously try not to use words or examples of things that are overtly culturally Christian. This isn't because I am ashamed of my faith; it is because an outsider does not get the metaphor or reference. I know words like *sanctify, redemption, justification,* and similar terms are important, but they are insider words and must be explained in a humble way to people who are not familiar. At our church, we also consciously avoid cultural Christian references and lingo. We aren't trying to be rebellious or snobby, but we are constantly focusing on evangelism and outreach. Going back to NMAC's Culture Wheel, how we speak either connects or puts distance between others and us.

3. I ask questions and listen more than I speak. I want to get to know them, not just talk about what I do. At the core of Christianity is the denial of self, and if we are going to minister to others, we must hear their story first. As they are speaking, I pay attention and look for opportunities to shine some light on whatever may be going on in their world. One of my biggest pet peeves is Christians, and especially Christian leaders, that talk too much. Our goal is to get to know others so we can build a deep relationship with them. That is impossible if we never shut up and listen. Though it is uncomfortable, I have had to have direct conversations with people I am discipling about how much they talk and how little they listen.

4. I look for common ground. Again, this is where the Culture Wheel becomes a powerful tool to connect with virtually anyone. Whether it is music, movies, art, sports, or whatever, I try and connect with people through simple commonalities. Many Christians may get uncomfortable with this, but the non-Christian music and movies I watch can be great conversation pieces to connect with non-Christians. This is why I encourage people not to confine themselves to just Christian entertainment. Of course, we don't allow things that can contaminate our hearts, but we need to know what the culture around us is watching, listening to, and being led by. If we don't know our hurdles, we will not be able to jump over them.

5. I am not looking to share my faith or what I do for a living in my first conversation. I don't believe in handing out tracts or walking up to strangers and asking if they need prayer. Does this work at times? Yes, but it's one in roughly 10,000 times that it works. The other 9,999 times, you just freak people the heck out. In my initial conversation, I just want to open the door. I want people to know that I am a normal guy with likes and dislikes and troubles just like anyone else. I want to bridge the gap between my world and theirs and hope that I can engage again on a deeper level sometime in the future. This doesn't mean that it is wrong to share your faith in the first conversation, but it should be a very natural progression. And it is best that they open the window for the conversation to take that turn.

God has placed opportunities all around us. There are people at your work that just need someone to reach out and say hello. There are students next to you that are struggling with depression and just need a smile or someone to eat lunch with. Your next-door neighbor may be going through a divorce, or your barista may be thinking of taking their life. We are called to be the salt and light, and sometimes the light starts to shine in a simple conversation over a cup of coffee. We need to be aware of the people around us, all around us! In a world that is increasingly narcissistic and closed off, we as the beacons of God's light must be willing to put down the phone, smile at those around us, and engage in some meaningful conversations. Does this make the seed grow? No, only God can do that, but it does plant seeds that we can come back to and water through more conversations.

TAKE AN INVENTORY:

1. Do you intentionally place yourself in situations that cultivate conversation with people you don't know?
2. Have you become so ingrained in cultural Christianity that you have forgotten how to talk to "normal" people?

CHAPTER 5

WHAT DOES IT LOOK LIKE TO BE A REAL PERSON?

"The culture that kept me here was the raw, unfiltered authenticity exemplified in things like talking about porn addiction from the stage—a general we-don't-need-to-play-games-here attitude."

—Jonathan Ciecka, Former atheist, now Project Manager at The Experience Community

If we are going to create authentic followers of Jesus Christ, we have to first be authentic. Going back to the opening chapter of this book, the culture bubble that Christians have created in the last thirty years has not been serving us well. We talk in a way that outsiders don't relate to. We isolate ourselves from people of different backgrounds, politics, and entertainment preferences. We have forgotten, as Paul says, to be "all things to all people" (1 Cor. 9:22). It isn't that the hearts of most Christians are bad, but that we have completely forgotten how to communicate with others outside of our comfort zone, especially non-Christians. Unfortunately, pastors can be the worst at this! If we are to create a personal culture that brings people into a healthy church culture, we have to find a way to connect with people who are different from us. This is impossible if we don't position ourselves to meet new people and if we don't have any way to start a meaningful conversation with them.

I have a hard time with 99 percent of Christian music and movies. In the spirit of honesty, I think we drop the ball in a major way when it comes to the arts. We don't make the best movies or music, and our attempts to compete in that market often just come up looking silly at best. Let's go back to my barista friend that I connected with over *Twin Peaks*. Now, I know what you older cats who remember the nighttime drama are thinking (spoiler alert): *What kind of pastor talks about a TV show about a promiscuous high school student that was murdered by her dad?* Well, of course we need to be very careful about what we watch, and we need to be acutely aware of the conviction of the Holy Spirit when it comes to what media we feed ourselves. But I also know that without some kind of connection to nonbelievers, we are at a great disadvantage when creating a relationship with them.

In the case with my Starbucks friend, a secular show became the launching pad to a great relationship. If I were to walk up to the same person and ask if he had given his life to Jesus Christ so that our Heavenly Father can justify him and lead him into sanctification by his grace, he would have just stared at me and thought I was nuts. We forget that people that haven't been properly introduced to our faith find it foolish and a little weird. Or if I had asked if he had paid $11 to see the new *God's Not Dead* movie, he would have chuckled at the idea of paying good money to see an overtly Christian film.

Maybe cult classic TV shows or wearing a David Bowie shirt isn't your best means of getting to converse with people, but perhaps you could talk sports, art, or business. The point is not to get all of you listening to the same music I do or watching *Twin Peaks*, but to find what connects you to the people around you in a very natural way. If we can show people that we value them and their life experiences, we can create a level of trust that can propel us into the next stage of relationship. Maybe conversation leads to coffee, coffee leads to seeing a movie, a movie leads to dinner with your family, and that dinner brings up faith. It may happen faster or it may take longer for God to show us the exact time to breach the topic of faith, but if we are faithful to plant and water, God will make something happen.

The danger of listening only to Christian music and watching only Christian movies is the loss of a connecting point with nonbelievers. One reason churches fail so much to reach the lost is that they use Christian means to attract non-Christians. Look, I am not advocating secular music in the church or doing cheesy movie-themed sermons. Our church doesn't do that nor will we ever, but when we are out and about in our daily lives, we cannot connect with the atheist college student over *God's Not Dead*, part 9. Those kinds of movies are made for Christians. This is why we don't bring Christian musicians, comedians, or movie stars into our church for events. Our events are geared both to equip the saints and also to be a connecting point for people to bring their unbelieving friend.

I honestly think that many Christians believe that God will just drop people in our laps. I remember a prayer one of the ministers would pray at the church that my wife and I got saved in. When he would come up to do announcements and pray before the preacher would speak, this minister would actually pray that the church would be so holy that people would just whip their cars around in the street and pull into the lot, not even knowing why they were doing it. This is nowhere biblically supported. Jesus sent his followers out to be "fishers of men." Last time I checked, fish don't just jump on hooks; they must be pursued.

Unfortunately, I think mainstream Christianity lives this idea that we just do our thing and people will come to us and ask why we are so great. Or we think wearing the t-shirt, slapping on the Christian bumper sticker, getting the Christian tattoo, or randomly walking up to people with a tract—but not taking the time to get to know them—will somehow grow the kingdom of God. It is clear to see by the rapid decline of the American church that our current methods are not working. If we are going to engage the broken world around us and see people become real disciples of Jesus, we are going to have to get into the mud and put some long-term work into getting to know, love, and lead people. It takes time, it is messy, and sometimes we may get hurt, but the work of the kingdom has never been easy.

God has created you to be you and you only. We live in a world that is screaming for something real, even though most people don't know what that looks like. The best thing we can all do is be what God has uniquely designed us to be. When we ask questions and get to know people a little bit better, we can more than likely find some kind of common ground that will eventually lead into the conversation of faith. But we must be real people. We must be vulnerable, be honest, and learn to function in a secular world. We must be overtly aware that isolation from people doesn't work, nor is it the heart of God. We must insulate ourselves with God's Spirit and pray for his wisdom. If we will be ourselves and rely on his help, we can create genuine and lasting relationships with people that don't live like we do.

How to Cultivate Authenticity

Now, I don't know exactly how to list out ways for someone to be authentic and real, but let me try.

1. Pray that God relieves you of the fear of what people think about you. Too many Christians care way too much about what others think about them. Of course, we need to have a good reputation, but God isn't looking for the coolest person. He is looking for dedicated followers that are trying to do his will above all other things.

2. Embrace who God made you to be. If you are a quirky Star Wars nerd, embrace that and talk about your nerdiness with the people that you come in contact with. Don't try to talk like the famous pastor or like hip cultural Christianity, don't get overly concerned with wearing what is in style, and don't try to fit every conversation into what is culturally in style. Just be you! We live in a time that longs for authenticity, and though we rarely get it, people desperately want and need it.

3. Share your frustrations and struggles (within reason). I think more people need to just be open about what they struggle with and what makes them upset. Of course, there are times, places, and people where this isn't always appropriate, but God's gift of wisdom can help you with that.

4. Admit when you're wrong and use it as a teachable moment. I often admit when I have made mistakes and need work. This shows others that I am a real person just like everyone else. Many people are afraid to show their weaknesses, or they take their weaknesses and make them their entire identity. However, I have found that people are much more apt to follow a real person that is honest with their struggles but doesn't use them as a crutch and way of escaping responsibilities.

Going back to the genesis of this book, recall that authenticity is where the church has greatly dropped the ball. We have overcompensated either by stressing the word *authenticity* more than the practice of it, or by burying our heads in the sand in fear of the world around us. We need to simply live what God has made us to be and use our uniqueness to connect with other unique people.

Look for Natural Ways to Share the Gospel

With all of this being said, we must get to a point with people when we share the Good News. If we feed all the hungry people, clothe all the naked, and love on all the broken without sharing with them the only message that will transform their lives and save their souls, we have failed. Though I am a proponent of loving others and applying the gospel to social

issues, I firmly believe that Christ came first and foremost
to save the souls of people (1 Tim. 1:15). Though the whole
point of the first part of this book is to build a bridge to talk
with and get to know others, the goal of that bridge is to walk
people across it to meet our Savior Jesus Christ. This is not
a bait and switch; this is the greatest love we can share with
others! Romans 10:17 tells us that faith comes from hearing
the Word of God. It is impossible for salvation and true change
to take place in broken people's lives unless we as born-again
Christians communicate it.

I think a great place to start is by telling people what God
has done for us. John wrote in Revelation Chapter 12 that
we overcome evil by the blood of Jesus and the word of our
testimonies, in other words by telling what God has done for
us. It is interesting that many of us start talking about the
Bible with nonbelievers in a way that assumes they would
hold that book in some kind of high regard. We often forget
that we can't expect non-Christians to act like Christians. It
is much more advantageous to get to know someone and then
share a personal story of redemption and life change. Though
the listener may not respect the Word yet, by this point they
probably respect you and are willing to take to heart what has
happened in your life. We should always be looking for natural
ways to insert our faith and what God has done in our lives
when conversing and getting to know people.

Fortunately, we are not alone in the work of getting people
to meet Jesus and then grow in their relationship with him.
Though I believe all of us can share our testimonies and the
gospel, and though I believe we can even lead people into a

relationship with Christ, we have a great weapon from God to aid us in this journey: the local church. As I quoted earlier, "The local church is the hope of the city." I believe this to be true. Yes, God is our salvation and hope, but he has chosen the church to be the instrument in his redemption of mankind. The importance and value of church community is paramount. I firmly believe that we are to lean into the church for growing the kingdom of God.

Even if we lead people into a relationship with Christ, the local church needs to be the next step in the evolution of the person looking to grow closer to God. If the people we have built relationships with are not yet at the point of conversion, the church should be a place where the seeking nonbeliever can come and be welcomed as they ask the hard questions of life and what comes after this life. Unfortunately, many churches have not been this source of refuge for the confused traveler. That's what the next chapters will discuss in greater detail.

TAKE AN INVENTORY:

1. How would you define terms like *authentic* and *genuine*? Would you say that you are an authentic and genuine person?
2. Do you believe Christians in the United States are good at having honest and deep conversations? How can we as Christians do a better job at being honest and "real"?

PART 2

WHAT HAPPENS IF THEY DO COME TO CHURCH?

The church is not the savior of mankind, but it is the greatest tool Jesus uses to communicate his message and bring people to himself, the true Savior. If we can create quality and genuine relationships with nonbelievers through a healthy personal culture that balances both biblical integrity and a welcoming environment, we can eventually lead them into a church community that hopefully has a healthy culture of discipleship. Hebrews 10:25 tells us that connecting to others and to God through the avenue of the church is not only important but grows in importance the longer we wait for Christ to come back. In a culture that underappreciates the value and role of the corporate body of believers, we need to be reminded just how important the local church is.

Unfortunately, the handoff from a person that has evangelized and built relationships through a healthy personal culture to many of the local churches in the United States is a scary one. The reason why is that many churches are not communicating and modeling the gospel the way Christ has called leaders to do. The tension of maintaining biblical integrity and a welcoming environment has been ignored or compromised, making the next step a shaky and intimidating one for people who are actively reaching the world around them.

We must also remember that the individual followers of Christ make up the church. Maybe we should stop passing all of the blame onto just pastors (though they will be held more accountable). All of us need to accept the responsibility for making an impact on the people that are around us all the time. Jesus didn't just commission pastors; he commissioned *all* followers to go out and make disciples, baptize, and teach. At the same time, it is true that church leaders have a large responsibility to create a church culture that both has integrity and welcomes all people to come and hear the Good News.

Again, I don't claim to have all the answers and methods that will instantly fix personal and church culture, but this section of the book will focus on the church leadership's role in some essentials the church must work on in order to change the perception and effectiveness of the Body of Christ. If you're not in official church leadership but love your church and want to see it be a place that welcomes all people while still holding onto biblical integrity, please continue to read and pray about sharing this with your pastor or whomever in church leadership is humble enough to welcome new ideas.

This list isn't an all-encompassing list that defines and steers through every intricacy of how a church community should function. It's a list of overarching principles that I believe every church needs in order to be the salt and light of their community. The church must be:

1. Authentic
2. Gracious

3. Community-Minded
4. Bible-Centered
5. Clear
6. Excellent

CHAPTER 6

THE CHURCH MUST BE AUTHENTIC.

"The thing that brought me to this church was the obvious culture of transparency and accountability. I noticed it from the start of coming to the church. As someone in my mid-twenties, it drove me to more honest relationships and it helped emphasize the importance of confession."

—Spencer Holloway, Videographer at The Experience Community

So what happens if more of us get to loving and getting to know the people that surround us every day at work, school, the gym, or the coffee shop? Is it enough to simply build a relationship with people without leading them into a next step? Well, no. If we truly love humanity, we want humanity to be saved by grace through their faith in Jesus Christ. Though it is not impossible for a person to be saved before attending a worship service, the best avenue to get people into an environment to hear and respond to the gospel of Christ is the local church.

Herein lies another monumental problem in the American church: it is dropping the ball when it comes to creating a culture that both welcomes the lost and fosters a genuine relationship with God (as I will keep saying in hopes of drilling this idea into our heads). We tend to go to extremes. We either create an incredibly welcoming environment that is mostly void of deep biblical teaching, discipleship, and moral integrity, or we so staunchly deliver the Word of God that we show no grace, creating an isolated Christian bubble that says to the outside world, "Change and then you are welcome to be in our community."

If we are to play the blame game, church leadership is mostly responsible for the opening section of this book. The church has not done a good job of equipping and encouraging its body to go out and engage the hurting world around them. We may hear pastors say things like, "We want this place to reek of weed, tobacco, and beer because so many lost people are here hearing the Word!" But in reality, churches don't really want the boat to be rocked so dramatically. If most leaders and congregants would be honest, we would admit that the path of least resistance is much more attractive than the dirty ditches we may have to climb into to save the "least of these." But before we get to sending people out into the ditches, how do we create a church culture that welcomes everyone but doesn't compromise the gospel?

About two years ago, I got one of the more interesting phone calls I have received since I started The Experience Community. One of the elders called me to tell me that a small group leader at our church had come out as a transgendered female and was about to go through the process of transitioning to a woman. Now, that isn't the shocking part. We have had many LGBTQ people come to our church over the years, but it was the person that really surprised me: a fifty-something-year-old man who had been married for over thirty years and was extremely successful in the automotive industry.

I immediately reached out to the individual and asked to meet over coffee. He agreed, and I very clearly told him how I felt and what the Bible says about gender and sexuality, but I also emphatically told him how much my wife and I along with our elders love him and will always welcome him. I promised him that the church would treat him well, even when he transitions. I told him that I will respect the fact that he wants to change his name and be referred to as a her, even though I didn't agree and didn't think it was what God wants for his life.

At first, my transitioning friend tried other houses of worship, especially gay- and trans-affirming ones all over the Nashville area, but eventually he came back to The Experience. Why? Because he felt valued, loved, and acknowledged even though we clearly did not agree with his lifestyle. He sends me a text almost every week encouraging me and telling me how much he loves the sermons and the community around him, and I still consider him a good friend.

I am almost positive that the last paragraph made a lot of you very uncomfortable. We have a Christian culture that elevates certain sins much higher than others, don't we? But let's not forget that there are people who would staunchly disagree with me allowing my trans friend to attend and worship with us, but who themselves lost their virginity before marriage and who struggle with greed and porn, and with hatred towards people different from them. I think we have moved away from the church being a hospital for the broken and hurting into more of a country club for people that wear thick masks of everything being all right. We dress up, we smile, and we tend to glide over the real issues in the world around us that are tearing families and individuals apart. We have got to start not only talking about the real obstacles of this life but allowing people that struggle with them to come in and hear the Good News that may change their lives.

I can't tell you how many times I have had people walk out on sermons because I openly talk about adult issues. Of course, I am not crass or vulgar, but we talk about sexual sin, idolatry of politics, and every other uncomfortable sin because it is what many people are struggling with. We will never get better until we acknowledge we have a problem. I have had to say to our very large congregation several times that this will always be a place where we talk about real issues. This is why we have excellent children's and middle school programs going on during our services and why I don't believe it is best to have all the family together in the sanctuary when I teach. We have age-appropriate teachings of the same Bible in those environments. But hey, if people are okay with their five-year-old hearing about Judges Chapter 19, where an old man cut up a concubine and mailed her pieces all over the place or hearing me teach the sexually charged book Song of Solomon verse by verse, that is their call. The point is this: the Bible touches on dark and sensitive issues and begs us to bring those sins and struggles to the surface.

Trickledown Authenticity

The authenticity has to start with the leadership and trickle all the way down to the parking lot team. The pastor of the local church needs to be a genuine person that communicates to the congregation his struggles and frustrations. Maybe the reason so many congregants wear masks is that they have learned from their pastor how to portray the shiny plastic façade that has unfortunately marked Christianity in America for way too long. We have way too many pastors that live way too comfortably and struggle to connect with the average person that comes into the church. We tend to talk, dress, and present ourselves in a way that really doesn't connect with the layman. We claim to have it all together, to never struggle with depression or fear, and to have perfect families and relationships. Maybe it is time to just be real.

I remember one time about a year ago, I told the congregation that I saw a counselor once a month because I deal with seasonal depression during the holidays. I had tons of people send emails or stop me in the grocery store and tell me how much it meant to them that I would be honest about my struggles because they also struggle with similar things. I had counselors call me and praise my bravery in telling the church the importance of counseling and mental health. I didn't know it at the time I said it, but it was kind of a landmark day in the maturation process of our church. But, like people can often do, someone strongly disagreed and sent me a nasty email. The email was a harsh criticism that I would be so open about my struggles. The message said I was a bad pastor because I didn't let God instantly deliver me from my seasonal depression and that I was a poor leader because I admitted weakness in front of thousands of people. I simply replied that this was a really bad church fit for her and her family because we value honesty over the façade that we are always okay. Needless to say, I never heard from her again.

The point is that the leadership should be authentic. They should be the same on Tuesday as they are on Sunday morning. This is why we all dress the same during our weekend services as we do during the week. Some may find that irreverent, but I disagree. In the summer, I never wear shoes because I almost always wear flip-flops, even when I preach on the weekends. During the video that plays between the worship and my message, I kick off my flip-flops and open my Bible in preparation to teach. Without fail, at every single Next Class (see Chapter 13) someone asks why I take off my flip-flops and teach barefooted. For years I never gave it much thought; I just hated wearing shoes and liked being myself in the pulpit. I remember one day a woman stopped me after service with tears in her eyes because it had hit her why I did the barefoot thing. She said, "Pastor, I figured it out. This is holy ground!" I really deflated her balloon when I said, "No, I just really hate shoes."

The reason I can justify barefoot preaching as not being irreverent is a story from a good friend of mine, a very successful real estate mogul named Bob Parks. Bob has almost 800 employees over a couple of states and is a very powerful, influential man in our community. Bob and his wife, Marie, have been attending our church for years, and he has become a good friend of mine. One day a woman from his office, who now comes to the church as well, told me that the reason she started attending The Experience Community was that Bob said it is the only place he can wear shorts, a t-shirt, and sandals. In other words, the church was the only place he could be himself 100 percent. It hit me how important my two-dollar flip-flops actually are. When we create an environment of authenticity and comfort, it allows people to let their guards down and focus on what is truly important: the Word of God and how he can penetrate our lives and change us. Maybe more people should kick off their shoes in church.

I heard another pastor say one time that the church will eventually look like the leadership. I believe this to be true. If the leadership puts on a façade that everything is okay all the time, the congregation will learn to lie. If the leadership fails to acknowledge their mistakes and struggles, it teaches the congregation to be arrogant. If the leadership dresses and carries themselves like movie stars, the congregation will learn to make more idols in their lives. When the Bible says that many shouldn't be teachers because they are judged more harshly (James 3:1), it isn't joking. The responsibility of leaders to set the bar and pace of authenticity is of the utmost importance. Please remember that God has made us all to be uniquely *us*. When we live in that honest and transparent spot, we not only honor God—we draw people into a community where they can also be themselves and let God heal what may be broken in their lives.

TAKE AN INVENTORY:

1. Why do you think leadership has such a hard time being 100 percent authentic?
2. What are some practical steps leaders can take to be more authentic?
3. What are the possible outcomes of authenticity in our churches?

CHAPTER 7

THE CHURCH MUST MODEL GRACE AND REDEMPTION.

"If I had started this church, I would have called it Hope Church, because everyone has access to hope here."

—Mike Lee, Small Groups Pastor and Development Team Lead

Several years ago, there was minor scandal in the church world in my community. A pastor that had been leading a thriving congregation had an extramarital affair and lost his church. Though I don't know every detail or how every person connected to that particular church treated the family and pastor, what I heard and witnessed is that they showed tremendous love and grace. Yet, even with all the love that was extended to the local pastor, his position had to be forfeited, and by his denomination's standards he would be forever ineligible to do vocational ministry.

I got an email from Pastor Mike about a year after the affair had been exposed. I had heard that Mike's daughter and son-in-law had been attending our church for a while, but Mike emailed me to tell me that he and his wife had started coming as well and that they loved the community. Whereas most pastors may have cautiously avoided getting too close to a guy with a tainted reputation like Mike's, I saw a tremendous opportunity to let grace and love be put on full display by allowing Mike not only to come but to be put back into a place of influence and even leadership. I remember him telling me that it caught him off guard how quickly I responded to his email and how happy I was the first time I met him in person. Mike isn't much of a crying type of guy, but he said when I told him how honored I was that he and his wife would attend our church, he broke down.

The first Christmas Mike and Dena were at our church, we asked Mike to do one of our Advent devotionals in front of all four services. It was about two years after his affair by that time, as well as the first time Mike had spoken to a full congregation since he was let go from pastoring his former church. Although nervous, he did a fantastic job. I remember getting on Facebook that weekend and seeing a pic from Mike's daughter of her dad speaking in front of thousands of people. She talked about how proud she was. Tons of people echoed her joy on the post. It was a cool moment of redemption, but not the last.

Mike did such a phenomenal job at Advent that we asked Mike to share his story at our church for a Men's Summit that we do every year. In front of hundreds of men, Mike opened up with, "I was a porn addict for thirty years, a liar, and I had an affair on my wife while I was a pastor of a church here in town." The crowd of men was absolutely stunned! My friend Bob was sitting next to me, and he broke out in laughter because he was overjoyed by the raw and blatant honesty with which Mike spoke. It was both breathtaking and exhilarating to hear such transparency from the stage. It was at that moment I knew I was going to hire Mike. I didn't know exactly where he was going to sit on the bus, but I knew I wanted him on it.

Hiring a former pastor that had a moral failure may seem nuts to a lot of people, but to The Experience, it made all the sense in the world. Our elders properly vetted and evaluated Mike, and once they saw the change and humility in him, they were just as excited as I was to bring him on board. Through it all, Mike has been a blessing to our community. Our bringing him on our team showed our church that we believe in redemption and second chances and that, though we may fall, we can all be put back to work for God's kingdom if we humble ourselves before him. If we are honest, how many of us have sinned but just haven't gotten caught? How many of us have been the woman lying on the ground as the crowd foams at the mouth at the idea of throwing stones at us? Isn't this where God shows up the strongest? Shouldn't the church model this?

So if we can agree that grace is a staple of Christianity and hopefully of the church, how can we model this in a way that is both authentic and healthy?

We can start by rewarding confession and punishing dishonesty. About six years into the life of The Experience, we had the budget to hire a full-time media and graphics person. We hired a young man that was immature in his faith and had also struggled with his sexuality. I knew all of this going in, and I was prepared to walk with him and help him grow spiritually as he worked for the church and grew as an artist and videographer. The young man made some pretty impressive videos and was great with people, but his sexual struggles would come and go and sometimes be a hindrance in his work performance. As you can see, our church has never shied away from hiring people with checkered pasts, but it was with this young man that we started to really push a policy that has become pivotal in our team: we reward confession and punish dishonesty.

After working at the church for a year or so, this young man came into my office and made a pretty hard confession. He had gotten on Craigslist and hooked up with three different older men, one being the father of a young woman in our church. I did my best to hold my tongue and not fly off the handle, but of course I was pretty mad and disappointed. After much prayer, I decided not to fire the young man. We put him on a probationary period where we had very tight accountability procedures and weekly check-ins. We paid for good Christian counseling and made sure, to the best of our abilities, that he would avoid future mistakes and actually grow in his faith despite his very bad decisions.

We also created a new policy. If anyone on staff is struggling with a sin, as long as it doesn't hurt others or break laws, and they confess that sin to me, we will not fire them. If it becomes chronic, of course we will have to ask people to forfeit their position for the sake of the reputation of the church and our faith. What this has created is not only an office environment that is honest and confesses sin; it has created a church culture that does the same because my staff has applied this process with their volunteers.

The point is to model grace. Of course, we should use wisdom and take time to properly assess people and their motives, but the church must be a place where ridiculous grace is shown. Yes, this needs to be handled with extreme wisdom and accountability. Grace without accountability becomes abusive and not in line with how God wants us to lead and live. But when we look at the example of Christ and the stories that range throughout the Word, grace is a constant and radical theme throughout the biblical narrative. We seem to talk about grace, and even point to the Scripture that says we are saved by it (Eph. 2:8), but when it comes to modeling it, we often drop the ball. We either go to the extreme of letting sin completely slide, or we absolutely destroy the person that has committed the offense.

I believe in both grace and biblical church discipline, and I also believe that the two work hand in hand. Proper discipline is not only a display of grace; it shows that we love people. Jesus even says in Revelation 3:19, "As many as I love, I rebuke and discipline." To walk the delicate line of grace and discipline, we must be in prayer, asking constantly for God's gift of wisdom. We must also have a clear path to put people back on, so they can truly be redeemed and worked back into a place of contributing to the kingdom of God.

Mike's story is a huge success. He was held accountable by a pastoral ministry, he attended church and submitted to the leadership, and he made significant life changes to avoid making the same mistake again. The nameless young videographer was not a success story, at least not yet. We took tons of measures to help him, but in the end he turned his back on the church, good relationships, and God. The reason I share this is to remind us that we cannot be held responsible for the results. We can plant and water like Paul told us to do, but the results are not ours. We are called to show grace, call out sin, and love and guide people on a path back to restoration, but we are not responsible for other people's decisions. This is a tough truth. I still struggle with it.

How your church models grace may look different from the two stories I shared in this chapter, but the point is clear: we are not only to teach the grace of God, we are to show it as well. My examples may be a bit extreme, but every day we have the opportunity to show grace and mercy to the people we influence. If we are ever going to connect with people that may be skeptical, apathetic, or even hurt, we must show them that we love them where they are and that we intend on helping them reach the place God wants them to be. Grace should be part of the DNA and be shown and modeled at every level of a church. If the congregation sees it from the stage, if the vocational leaders train their volunteer leaders on how to show both wisdom and grace, and if volunteer leaders show it to volunteers, grace will become a staple of the local church and will permeate throughout the community at large.

TAKE AN INVENTORY:

1. Do you know any remarkable stories about a church showing grace to someone that did something awful? What was the outcome of that grace?
2. How can we as Christians better balance grace and discipline within the church?

CHAPTER 8

THE CHURCH MUST BE COMMUNITY- AND PURPOSE-MINDED.

While I was working on this book at a local coffee shop, a children's book author that comes to our church came in and we started to talk a little about the writing process. He asked what this book was focusing on, and I told him it was about the culture of Christians and the church. He instantly jumped in and said the thing he loved the most about our church was the vision and how giving to our church is not just about our church, but that our church has become a funnel to help community programs and nonprofits all over middle Tennessee.

We are all working for something bigger than just our church, city, state, or even nation. We are working for the eternal kingdom of God! In Jesus' Sermon on the Mount, he even tells us that our reward is in heaven, not on this earth. I know that most Christians know that, but we rarely meditate on his words and live in such a manner. I think if we did a better job as leaders communicating the kingdom, we could get more people involved in every level of growing that kingdom.

This generation is motivated more by purpose than money, and somewhere along the line I think the church failed to present the fact that we have the most important purpose in the world: being the salt and light of our communities. We are told to be a light on a hill that illuminates the entire area. I believe that most local churches have a part in that light, but we often do a poor job of communicating that to the people that attend our services. If we are not strategic about showing the values of the church to the congregation, or if our values are not in alignment with God's, the culture of the church will not be one that makes authentic followers of Christ.

The clearest way we communicate what The Experience Community values is through our Vision Services that we have twice a year. I not only tell the church where I think God is leading us; I give them clear and precise budget numbers on where the hard-earned money that they give is going. The congregation has actually fallen in love with these Vision Services. They love to see that 20 percent of our annual budget is going out of our church into community service projects. We support dozens of nonprofits, we support multiple churches in New England, and we do long-term missions in other countries. They appreciate that our salary percentage is almost 15 percent lower than the average church salaries in the United States and that they can trust us with their tithes. It isn't all about money, but how a church uses its finances shows what the church ultimately values. We show them our goals for the year and ask them to keep us accountable. We push our small groups and serving opportunities in the hopes that they will understand that we value their walk with Christ and the road they are walking on as they grow closer to him.

The point is this: what the church consistently puts in front of their congregation will be what the congregation ultimately values. If the church spends a majority of its budget on gimmicks, fancy lights and sound, and production technology, the congregation will learn to think those things are essential to making the church experience worth engaging in. If the church consistently pushes events with celebrity speakers instead of community service projects and with softball teams before discipleship classes, the church will learn to value things that are not really the main focus and mission of what God wants the church to be.

Serving the Community

We live in a time of extreme self-centeredness. We've come a long way from the days of Henry Ford proclaiming that people can get his cars in "any color as long as it's black" to a time when we can virtually customize everything to our liking. Of course, there are great advantages to the freedom of design and accessibility that we enjoy in our day and age, but like most things in American culture, we have proven that we cannot do many things with balance and moderation. This overindulgence of self-expression and customizable everything has not only damaged genuine and healthy communities in the world but has greatly affected the culture of the Church. If the church is going to create an environment that releases true disciples of Jesus, we must make sure that our culture is one of genuine servitude to each other and our community.

One of the negative effects of being immersed in a culture of self-centeredness is our growing sense of entitlement. This sense has led us into an almost complete void of empathy for others. This lack of empathy has led us into a mindset that we are here to be served, not to serve others. Now, I know you may be thinking, *Wait, isn't this one of the most purpose- and cause-oriented generations in centuries?* On paper, this is true, but if we go one step deeper into the hearts of people in our age, we find that the heart is still in a place of depravity. Many serve, but only the cause that is convenient for them, only the organization they start, or only the people that never challenge their ideals or address their faults. So what has happened is we have created a way to serve in order to ultimately serve ourselves.

Of course, this self-service is nothing new. People have been hiding self-centeredness under the blanket of servitude since the beginning of civilization. Jesus talks about this in Matthew 20 when it becomes clear that even some of the disciples were serving with the wrong motives. Jesus replies to them,

You know that the rulers of the Gentiles lord it over them, and those in high position use their authority over them. It must not be this way among you! But whoever wants to be great among you must be your servant. And whoever wants to be first must be your slave—just as the Son of Man did not come to be served but to serve (Matt. 20:25–28a).

Jesus also warned his disciples when he said that if we seek the reward of people, there is no reward from God (Matt. 6:1). The point is pretty clear: we are to serve for the sake of God and others, not for ourselves. Ironically, there is a great reward for us as individuals if we serve with proper motives. Though it should never be about us, God does bless and exalt those that serve for no other reason but the glory of God and the benefit of others.

Unfortunately, we have started looking at the church similarly to how we perceive corporations and service industries in the world. Many people who have been immersed in church culture have such an unhealthy (I would say nauseating, but that's not nice) perception of the church as a place to simply serve their needs with no obligation of ever contributing back into the mission of the church. I have had so many conversations with congregants who complain about everything from the temperature of the coffee to the height of the walls in the nursery (they were too short for their liking).

Somewhere down the line, people have taken their free coffee, childcare, message, and all of the other programs and resources and have assumed that they are owed the luxuries. They begin to assume that these are the things that church is for, that the church is for them to consume and leave happy so they can trudge through another week. What an entitled and selfish culture we have allowed to flourish in our churches! Quite frankly though, churches are the ones to blame. For decades now, we have made this an environment of professionals whose job is to entertain the crowds as long as they tithe and fill seats. We have made the house of God into a Las Vegas dinner show.

During my time as the pastor at The Experience Community, I have often gone through times of battling hard feelings toward the church at large. Not toward our church, but toward church culture as a whole that sometimes weasels its way into our local congregation. John F. Kennedy said it best in his inaugural speech: "Ask not what your country can do for you—ask what you can do for your country."[5] This line of thought needs to be taught to the modern church. Granted, there is a time when a new Christian consumes in a childlike manner. Yet, as we have seen with the original twelve disciples, we consume for a time, but then we grow up spiritually and are able to start pouring out the knowledge and wisdom that has been graciously given to us through his Spirit. One of the ways we pour back out is in service and giving to the local church and our community.

So what is the paradigm shift that needs to take place when it comes to serving? How do we create a culture of discipleship by how we teach and serve? The answer involves both the hands and heart.

1. What does "serving others" even mean? Serving people is not just going on mission trips or giving out food for the homeless community. These are noble and needed things. But I often see that we make a hierarchy of good deeds. To borrow a metaphor from the Bible, we tend to say to the nose that, because we are an eye, we are more important to the kingdom. I also notice that people tend to flock to very visible social causes, but few people want to prepare 3,000 communion cups for weekend services, clean up the parking lot, or pack the bags that are given out to needy families in the neighborhood. Why? Because there is little to no recognition in it. We need to remember that disciples of Jesus live a lifestyle of service. This means we adopt an attitude that is happy to serve other people. If someone needs help at the copier at work or your wife needs the kitchen cleaned or the delivery guy needs the door held open, and so on, you receive it as an opportunity to serve. You get the picture; we are to live in service to others for the greater good of the community and to glorify God.

2. Are we serving others? What are you doing on a consistent basis to serve the people around you? Do you give financially to the church or to nonprofits? Do you block off time to dedicate to helping at your kids' school? Perhaps you could help prepare for the weekend service, get someone's coffee at work, go the extra mile for your spouse, feed the poor, go on mission trips, or even mow your neighbor's yard. When I hear people complain, I often ask, "What are you doing to make our city, nation, or world a better place?" Anyone can tell you what is wrong, but it takes a leader and servant to go out and make a change!

3. Why are we serving others? Here is where the heart issue comes into play. What is your motive for serving? Do you want everyone to know how great you are? Do you want that epic picture on your Instagram of you holding a malnourished child from a foreign country? Do you want to satisfy some moral insecurity in yourself that may come from bad choices? I am not trying to be a sarcastic jerk, but we need to be honest with ourselves. Many of us have heart issues that lead us to serve for our benefit and not the kingdom's.

When it comes to Christians serving nonbelievers, we must remember that we serve for their benefit, and that the ultimate goal is to see people come to Christ. But regardless of the outcome, we are called by our Creator to serve and to serve with pure motives. Though service with improper motives may have some positive outcomes, the potential long-term damage to our faith and our reputation with others could greatly cripple the church if it hasn't done so already.

4. Are we humble enough to go to the need, not our want? Most often, people do not care about the needs of the church as much as their desire to do a specific service. Now I understand that we want people to serve where their natural talents and strengths are, but we also need to steer people to want to meet the needs of the congregation and community more than their personal desires to do a ministry that they feel passionate about. The point is that the greater good of the kingdom of God trumps our personal preferences. Like most things within the Christian faith, it boils down to whether or not we have humility. When we remain humble and focused on the needs of the local church and community, we not only honor God, but I believe we will eventually get the opportunity to do the things we are passionate about. It is the men and women who ask, "What does the Body of Christ need?" that I enjoy working with the most.

5. Do we respect the authority and wisdom of others? Maybe one of the most frustrating parts of leading a younger congregation like The Experience is the lack of respect in younger generations for older people and authority in general. There is a problem of epidemic proportions with younger generations when it comes to respecting authority, and unfortunately Christians have not been immune. The prophet Zechariah wrote, "Who dares despise the day of small things?" (Zech. 4:10, NIV), a passage I quote quite often. I'm reminded that the person who despises small tasks will never be trusted with large ones. When we lack respect for those who have paved the way before us, and when we become so arrogant as to think others cannot offer helpful insight, we are on the verge not only of failure but of hindering God's blessings on our lives. As of right now, I lead a church of 3,000 people, but when I talk to any leader, regardless of how large or small their sphere of influence is, I respect them and listen to the ideas they have to give. For example, we work with a church in New Hampshire that is around 200 people, but they do things very well. As we are helping them, I often glean many great ideas from what they do. In fact, they have been doing ministry a lot longer than I, and they have some really good insight on how to serve and lead others.

As always, Jesus is the perfect example. In John 13:12–15, Jesus responds to the shock of his disciples after he washed their feet:

When Jesus had washed their feet and put on his outer clothing, he reclined again and said to them, "Do you know what I have done for you? You call me Teacher and Lord—and you are speaking rightly, since that is what I am. So if I, your Lord and Teacher, have washed your feet, you also ought to wash one another's feet. For I have given you an example, that you also should do just as I have done for you."

Jesus came to serve, not to be served (Mark 10:45), and as his followers, imitators, "little Christs," we are to act as much like Jesus as possible. I know the passage of Jesus washing Peter's feet is used very often for a multiplicity of lessons, but the clearest one is the lesson of servitude to your fellow man.

If the God of the universe that came down to earth to die for our sins can take off his robe and wash the dirty feet of one of his creations as an act of service, we can do some proverbial foot washing with people in our community too! The act of washing feet was a precedent that Christ was setting. He was essentially saying, "Go out and get dirty helping those around you!" This isn't about getting stained by the world, but about being humbled and filled with joy as we get to imitate Jesus in how we serve others. One of the greatest ways we can own our identity as a "chosen race, a royal priesthood, a holy nation, a people for his possession, so that [we] may proclaim the praises of the one who called [us] out of darkness into his marvelous light" (1 Pet. 2:9) is to serve others with love. Why? Well, because Christ has not only served us but saved us by his grace and mercy.

When is the last time you washed someone else's feet? Of course, I don't mean this literally, although there is nothing wrong with foot washing ceremonies. But you get the point. When is the last time you put your pride aside and served someone in the most humbling way? Every day, we have the opportunity to do small things that speak volumes to those around us. Have you run errands for your coworker, bought lunch for your friend, sacrificed your place in line, or made any kind of conscious effort to put others above yourself lately?

In Acts Chapter 13, we see the climate of the church in Antioch. Antioch was a hedonistic, mostly Greek and Roman city that was on the cutting edge of culture and arts. But unlike the hedonistic culture around it, the church in Antioch longed to serve the world. Led by Barnabas, Paul, Lucius, Simeon, and Manaen, the church was preparing to launch out into other parts of the world unreached by the gospel. How did they know what to do and how to do it? They prayed and fasted, and the result was a series of church planting journeys which redirected the trajectory of an empire.

I recently taught through Acts Chapter 13, and I found myself getting upset, almost depressed, at the state of the modern church. We wonder why we have such a turnover of congregants and why the depth of their maturity in Christ is so shallow. The reason is that the leadership of the church has created such a monster of consumerism and shallow faith by pandering to people in order not to lose them to church X down the street. Furthermore, we have young leaders that don't want to submit to any authority, so they plant more churches in areas that are oversaturated, and the problem continues even further.

The culprit is us. We have moved so far from what the primary functions of the Body should be that we have become something that would be completely foreign to the first-century church. We have tried to doll up the Bible with surface-level sermon series. We have virtually no church discipline. In the process, we have lost sight of discipleship and, quite frankly, the entire Great Commission of Jesus.

TAKE AN INVENTORY:

1. How are you serving your community?
2. How does serving the community open the door for discipleship?
3. How has the church at large succeeded and failed in the arena of servitude? How about your local church?

CHAPTER 9

THE CHURCH NEEDS TO LEAN MORE INTO THE BIBLE.

"The mission of our church is to build authentic followers of Jesus Christ, and that is evident in the entire culture of the church. The day I stepped foot into the church (June 2017 to be exact) I realized something was different. Corey and all the leaders of our church do not sugarcoat the Bible to please society; they teach pure truth."

—Julia Baldree, Accountant at The Experience Community

The greatest way to cultivate a culture that is welcoming to all kinds of people while still holding onto biblical integrity, is to, well, hold on tight to the Word of God. Going back to something I said earlier in the book, pastors and leaders from churches all over the country call our offices, drop by unannounced, or set up time for their elders and teams to meet with me or others on my team. They want to find out what we are doing that grew the church and created such an environment that virtually anyone would feel comfortable in. They ask about how we marketed (which we never have) or how we do large-scale events (of which we do very few). They want to know about the décor, the lighting, the sound, and song selection, but when I finally give them one of the biggest reasons why I think our culture has been so successful, you can almost see the color drain from their faces.

Now, don't get me wrong, there is a lot more to creating a culture than any one element. But the first thing I always go back to as the main source of our church's success is how we teach and communicate the importance of the Bible. I am a firm believer in expository teaching (going line by line through the Word) because it forces the pastor and the congregation to lean into the transcendent principles and culture of God rather than the fleeting and temporal principles of our modern culture. Modern church culture desperately attempts to make the Bible more appealing, which only cheapens the power and authority of the Scriptures.

At the beginning of this book, I stated that the insider talk of Christians actually makes me angry. This is no exaggeration. I actually get mad, sometimes to the point that I need to repent. The pinnacle of my anger comes when I see the lame attempts of pastors to create sermon series that, in my opinion, cater more to first graders than they would to grown, educated adults. The problem is that many Christian leaders really don't think the Word is enough. They would never admit this, but they live it. They subconsciously believe that no one would come to a five-month series on Ecclesiastes, so they doll up the Scripture with some cheesy slogan and teach brief snippets of the Word, while their funny life stories fill the majority of the lesson. Again, they would never admit it, but they present the Word in bite-sized chunks because at their core they don't think it will draw the masses. I want to push back on that, and in a very major way!

In the eleven years The Experience Community has existed, we have never taught from the pulpit any other way except chapter-by-chapter expository teaching. This has had a number of positive effects on our rapidly growing congregation.

1. It has taught the congregation to love the Word. Teaching the Bible in a very systematic way (chapter-by-chapter) instills in our congregation a love for reading God's Word. Similar to a television show that comes on the same time every week, the books of the Bible, when taught with passion and intentionality, become something that draws the readers in and inspires them to learn more. I love hearing people talking about not only how they read the Bible with more consistency but also how much they are learning and applying it to their lives.

2. It has taken the fear out of reading the Word. Most people never attempt to get into the Bible because they are terrified of it. Let's show some grace here; it is a huge and powerful book! We should have some trepidation when approaching the Bible, but not to the point of never reading it. By walking through whole books of the Bible week in and week out, the church sees that the Word of God is not only digestible but that the layman can tackle the Bible and get a lot from it.

3. It has put the Word into proper context. One of the things that bothers me more than almost anything is when the Bible is taken out of context. I came from a denomination that would twist and manipulate small passages of Scripture in order to fit certain ideological leanings or whatever was making the pastor angry that week. By teaching whole chapters and whole books over a longer period of time, we are able to put the teachings of the Bible into proper and understandable context. This protects the church from bad theology and steers people into a deeper understanding of their Savior.

4. It tackles the hardest issues. Maybe one of the reasons many churches don't lean into the Bible more is that the Word can be extremely offensive to some of the hot button issues of our time. When one goes through 1 Corinthians, for example, they are going to come to some very controversial passages that hit at the core of humanity's struggles. The beauty of leaning more into expository teaching is that these tough conversations cannot be avoided. We must dive into the deep end and talk about the mess!

5. It puts the pressure on a God that can handle it versus people that cannot. The most beautiful thing for me about teaching through the Word is that, when we do come across difficult passages that address controversial topics, I can lean on God and let him take the heat. For example, when the Word brings up greed, materialism, same-sex relationships, or any other tough topic, I can fall back and say, "This is not my idea or command; I am just called to follow what God tells us to do."

Leaning into the Word of God should give us clarity on the topic of the next chapter: making the priorities of the church crystal clear. Looking back, the Bible should also bring clarity to the previous chapter: the church must be community- and purpose-minded. The Bible is the mind of

God on paper. It is our clearest and most conclusive way to know what God is telling his church to do. The Bible shows us what God values—and knowing what God values teaches us what we as a church should value. If we will consistently turn back to the Word of God for guidance and help, our churches and the people in them will look more like the church that he wants us to be.

TAKE AN INVENTORY:

1. If you are a pastor or small group leader, or are discipling an individual, are you leaning on the Word more than any other resource?
2. Why do you think so many pastors shy away from expository teaching?
3. Though supplemental books are not bad, what is the danger of primarily reading and studying books other than the Bible?

CHAPTER 10

THE CHURCH MUST MAKE THE PRIORITIES OF THE CHURCH CRYSTAL CLEAR.

"We were drawn to the way that this church truly lives out the gospel by serving the marginalized in society, preaching the Word and not an agenda, being good stewards of resources, handling conflict biblically, and remaining true to our simple mission of making authentic disciples of Jesus. Our first impressions of this church have remained true and this community has welcomed us as family faster than any other church we've been a part of. We are so grateful to call this place home."

—Amanda Keener, Student Pastor at The Experience Community

If we are going to move people through the progression of becoming authentic followers of Christ, we must be clear on the road that leads them to where we—and, more importantly, God—want them to go. A book that absolutely changed my life was *Simple Church* by Thom Rainer and Eric Geiger.[6] In the last eleven years as The Experience has grown from three people in 2009 to over 4,500 in over three campuses in 2020, keeping things simple has been extraordinarily difficult! But keeping things simple at 200 people can be just as difficult, as some of our smaller campuses are finding out. People have selfish agendas; they want this and that, but our job is not to be an all-encompassing one-stop shop. Our goal is to make disciples, baptize them, and teach them what the Lord has shown us through his Word.

Majors and Minors

Every month, usually on the second Monday, we have all the newer people in our church come to what we call the Next Class. This is an informal tour of the facilities plus some coffee, and I tell my testimony and the story of the church. We also follow up the testimony with questions they may have regarding how we do things. Almost every month, someone asks about my statement that we "major in the majors and minor in the minors." This statement simply means that we divide theological conversations into two camps: things that are essential to salvation (major), and things that are theological but not essential for salvation (minor).

I think most people who have been in church for almost any length of time can tell you that our faith has been divided, sometimes viciously, over things that are not essential to people going to heaven. We have friendships and church splits over questions such as predestination or free will, casual attire or formal, instruments or acapella, whether one can lose salvation, pews or chairs, deacons or elders, how we do communion, or a slew of other topics that are not hills to die on. If some of the things in this list sound like nonessential things that aren't worth damaging relationships over, I would challenge you to believe that all of them are! Though our church talks about predestination, free will, elders, and so on, these are not topics that we allow to divide the congregation in our church. These things are minors.

If Christianity is going to progress, we must get back to the core of what we are to do. Jesus, in Matthew 28:19–20, gave us the Great Commission, which is essentially his vision statement as to what his followers were to do after he ascended into heaven. In the Great Commission, Jesus states that we are to "make disciples, baptize, and teach" and that he would be with us "to the end of the age." We as a faith community must focus first on the things Jesus focused on: making followers of Jesus that make more followers of Jesus, baptizing them into the family of God, and teaching them the Word of God. Here are some of the majors we focus on at The Experience Community:

1. The Deity and Exclusivity of Jesus as God. We must be very clear in who we believe God to be. We live in a time that has become increasingly pluralistic, and if the Christian church is to advance God's kingdom, we must be clearer than we have ever been about who created that kingdom and who rules it for eternity. Though I believe most churches agree with this at their core, many have started to prioritize interreligious activities in which evangelism is increasingly suppressed as something which is unnecessary and distasteful. Likewise, many have remained shockingly quiet on the exclusivity of salvation through Christ alone. Many churches have also gone to great lengths to humanize Jesus more than illuminate his deity. As followers of Jesus and potential leaders of his church, we must be clear in where we stand lest our denial on earth lead to his denial of us in the next life (Matt. 10:32–33).

2. The Cross and Resurrection. We need not only to consistently remember the redemptive act of the cross but to teach why Christ would do such a thing for us. One of the ways we keep our minds constantly on the cross at our church is through communion (see below). And just as Jesus' resurrection was central to the early church's message, so too is Jesus' resurrection the foundation for our hope at The Experience.

3. Repentance. The Bible teaches that one must not only confess and ask forgiveness for things that are contradictive to God's instruction, but that we must turn from a life of sin. It is unfortunate that many modern churches have moved away from a clear message of repentance. I am not a proponent of "fire and brimstone" scare tactics, but I do find it extremely important to remember that Jesus said in Matthew 4:17, "Repent, because the kingdom of heaven has come near." Without repentance of sins, there is no gospel of Jesus Christ! Unfortunately, most of the more charismatic movements in America talk so frequently of God's love, grace, healing, and power that we rarely hear that repentance is the catalyst for a relationship with God. Without changing how we think and act, there can be no authentic relationship with God.

4. Baptism. This reenactment in water of the death, burial, and resurrection of Jesus tells the world that we are taking on the identity of Christ. We do our best not to brag on the rapid growth of The Experience Community, but we are not shy about pointing out our baptism numbers. To us, this is true growth and success for the church. Though some churches may debate the mode, timing, and symbolism of baptism, I think the consistent teaching of the baptism experience is a major component of the Christian walk.

5. Discipleship. This is where the church as a whole is failing the worst. We American Christians have created great houses of entertainment, good speaking, catchy sermon series, and elaborate buildings, but we haven't done a great job of making disciples who make more disciples. A conversation in 2016 with Jim Putnam, the author of *Real-Life Discipleship*,[7] completely changed the entire trajectory of our church. Though we were already in the same mindset as far as community, our church was not being as intentional about making followers of Jesus that went and made more followers of Jesus. This is the core of what Christ commanded us to do, yet so few churches do it. This major point may be the underlining current of this book. The lack of true biblical discipleship is the most detrimental failure the church has made because all the other major points in this list get ignored if discipleship is not a priority in the church.

6. Communion. As I mentioned earlier, one of the ways we keep our minds on the cross is through communion. We aren't militant about how we take it, but we take it every service with repentant hearts. It is a time for us to reflect, and regardless of what the topic that week is during service, we always go back to the cross. The method and frequency are minors to us, but whether or not we take time through communion to remember what Christ has done for us is a major. This is such a beautiful and important instruction that Christ himself gave his followers.

7. Community. We heavily teach that God is a communal God that wants us to be active in the local church community, and also in the community at large. Though the church is rarely at the center of the city geographically anymore, we should be working to be at the center of the city in our involvement, service, and improvement as much as possible. As I have said on more than one occasion in this book, I am convinced that the local church is the hope of our communities.

8. Community Service. The last step of our discipleship process at The Experience is serving. We are not saved by good works, but we are not saved from them either. We are called to respond to the world around us because God has saved us by his grace. Many churches get involved in good works, but few put their money where their mouth is. The local church should be using their hands *and* their wallets to make an impact on their community. I suggest that every church should begin with 10 percent benevolence and grow into greater percentages. We are currently at 20 percent.

9. The Gifts and Fruit of the Holy Spirit. This is not to elevate certain gifts over others, but we constantly teach that the Spirit of God still fills us and empowers us to live in a way that is beyond our abilities. We stand strong on the fact that God still imparts his gifts to his followers and that we should produce the fruit of the Spirit in our daily lives. In 1 Corinthians Chapter 12, Paul tells us to not be unaware of the giftings God has shared with us, so that we can both edify the church and build up our relationship with him.

These examples are what I and our church as a whole consider overarching things that the church as an organization should really focus on. Churches have gotten so sidetracked by things that are not imperative to people's souls being saved that we have largely forgotten the most important things.

This forgetfulness plays out in our interactions with other people. When it comes to our personal interactions, we have to learn to pick our battles wisely. For instance, if you engage in a conversation with a woman whose life is falling apart due to infidelity and chronic sexual deviance, but your first priority is to make sure she stops smoking cigarettes, you may have gotten your minors and majors confused. Though smoking is addictive and destructive to one's body, in dealing with someone who feels utterly broken, we need to deal with the majors first: Does this woman know you care for her and will walk with her through her pain? Does she know who Jesus is and what he did for her even while she was sinning?

We have also wasted so much time amongst Christians debating things that are not essential to souls being saved. Because of this, churches often don't work well together, if they work together at all. We let minor issues divide our congregations while the majors of our faith slip off into obscurity. We wonder why Christianity in America is shrinking, but we fail to see that we have been so busy making sure the makeup looks good that we neglect to check if our hearts are even beating properly. We are slowly dying because our focus has become myopic. If we are to create a culture that makes true disciples of Jesus, we must spend our energy working on teaching and modeling the major objectives of our faith.

I often tell our congregation that I can look at a person's usage of time and money and tell them what they love and how they prioritize. I think Christians and churches need to lift the hood on how we use our time and money and be honest about what we really find to be valuable to us. Not what *should* be valuable, but what actually is revealed to be valuable to the church based on where we put our resources. The reason I am bringing up time and money is that the church (by this, I mean all Christians combined) has let minors take priority over majors. So we wonder why we lose relationships with other believers that have minor differences with us and why we don't connect or build bridges with nonbelievers over things that are nonessential to salvation. It's because we have built a Christian culture based around valuing the wrong things.

How do these dots connect? Well, if congregations spend the majority of their money on buildings, advertising campaigns, celebrity worship leaders, and all the bells and whistles of the latest production and tech equipment, we will miss the real focus of the church: making disciples, reaching the lost with the gospel, and serving the community. Do I have a problem with advertising or having a quality livestream for services? Of course not! But whenever a church puts more money into production than community service and missions or when the vision of the church centers on the building campaign and not the advancement of the gospel, a clear message is sent: "We care more about us than them." It creates

a mindset, and one that I would argue values minors more
than majors.

So what do we do? Again, I don't have all the answers, but
change always starts with the individual. I recommend we all
take an inventory of where our personal time and money go.
If we are not faithful with giving tithes to the church, we don't
believe in the vision and mission of the church as much as we
may say. If our time is spent in selfish ways and not in serving,
praying, investing into others, or pouring over the Word, we
may not be as close to Christ as we have deceived ourselves
into thinking we are.

Church leaders must also be more transparent. We
must be showing our congregations what we are doing with
resources and what our plan is for using them to greater
efficiency. Church leaders are stewards over God's money and
God's people's time. I believe the church also needs to know
when enough is enough. We need to be the most frugal of all
organizations, and we need to find balance when it comes to
how we use the resources of the congregation.

The bottom line is this: we must let the small things be
small things, and we must give the big things our best. God
has trusted all of us with much, and we must use well all that
we are loaned from him. When it comes to other brothers
and sisters in the faith, don't let the small things burn bridges.
This is foolish and not Scriptural. When we interact with
nonbelievers, we must minister to them with majors that
will impact their eternities, not minors that can be left up to
debate. The goal is not to win an argument, but to win people
to the kingdom of God! Remember, the culture of the church

will be determined by what it values. Do we value *people* more than the minor ideological differences others may have?

Fundamental Church Objectives

I think we also need to dive deep into the Word and seek God in prayer to make sure that we are focusing our efforts on the most fundamental objectives of the church. Is our church culture in line with the culture God wants our churches to demonstrate to the world around us? For years now, we at The Experience have focused on a small list of things that we should make the highest priority in our churches. Everything we do steers people to practice these fundamentals. In fact, I was teaching a class recently to a group of guys that I hope will all be pastors one day. I told them that I really only talk about a handful of things, but in different ways and at different times. Why? Because the fundamentals of the church are constant, and the need for the church to be reminded of them is constant.

1. Prayer and Fasting. Modern church culture has almost perfected environments, music, production, attractive architecture, and the presentation of the Word through visuals and object lessons. We have created groundbreaking programs, apps, and software, and we have created leadership conferences that rival any in the corporate world. But Jesus didn't want us to build houses of music, of leadership development, or even of good teaching. He asked us to build a *house of prayer.* Oddly enough though, this is one of the hardest ministries for churches to gain traction in. If the church is to become truly healthy and grow in the ways God wants us to, we have got to get back to a place of prayer and fasting.

2. The Great Commission. With people, especially lots of people, the natural progression is toward greater complexity. I think the church has fallen into this trap in a major way. Though Jesus is complex in who he is, his core message and instruction to us is quite straightforward and simple: disciple, baptize, and teach. The mission of the church should be to fulfill these three simple instructions from God. We need to be asking ourselves with every new program, every expansion, and every dollar spent: *Does this move us toward the Great Commission?*

3. Gathering Together to Worship. Weekly church attendance has become a double-edged sword of sorts. Many nominal Christians use their weekly attendance at church as their "get into heaven free" card, though their lives throughout the week do not reflect in any way the things they heard on the weekends. On the other hand, many people claiming to be followers of Christ are attending church less frequently. In my experience, people's spiritual, emotional, and relational health is almost, if not always, synonymous with their church attendance. In other words, when professing Christians don't make coming to church on a weekly basis a priority, their lives start to fall apart. This is why the author of Hebrews encouraged "not neglecting to gather together, as some are in the habit of doing, but encouraging each other, and all the more as you see the day approaching" (Heb. 10:25). Coming to church is important! Not for the numbers or the bragging rights of the pastors, but so that people can recharge by hearing the Word, worshiping with other like-minded believers, and taking communion to remember the sacrifice of the Savior.

4. Reading the Bible. I came from a church that professed a love for the Word, but we taught very little from it. We would take one or two verses that, if twisted just right, would fit our narrative of whatever soapbox we wanted to climb upon that week. The Bible was used more as a manipulation tool than the instruction of the Lord for our lives. Maybe the reason more Christians don't read the Word is that few pastors teach from it. We have done such a poor job of communicating the importance of knowing the Bible that now we are paying a high price for people's lack of biblical knowledge. We as individuals need to have intentional time in our lives when we read and study God's Word, and churches need to get back to teaching through books of the Bible and putting a lot of effort into creating a more biblically literate church.

5. Giving to the Mission of the Church. When the church was birthed in Acts Chapter 2, one of the major characteristics of the church was sacrificing property and possessions in order to meet the needs of others in the community. This trend continues all throughout the New Testament, as more established churches would collect money to distribute during times of famine and hardship. We also see the benevolence of Christians such as Lydia who believed in the missionary work of Paul, as well as whole churches like the one in Philippi that were known for their giving and financial contribution to the advancement of the gospel and social justice in their region and beyond. We are to be givers, not just of time, but of our finances. My pastor at the Pentecostal church where I was saved always told me that we can live better on 90 percent than we ever can on 100 percent because we are trusting God with our money.

6. Serving the Local Community. As I said before, we are not saved by our works, but we are not saved from them either. Christians are not only commanded to serve; serving is modeled to us by Christ himself: "Just as the Son of Man did not come to be served, but to serve, and to give his life as a ransom for many" (Matt. 20:28). We should be so humbled by the grace that God has bestowed upon us that we have a natural desire to respond with loving and serving those around us: "Heal the sick, raise the dead, cleanse those with leprosy, drive out demons. Freely you received, freely give" (Matt. 10:8). Although this verse is in reference to the power of the Holy Spirit working through us, the point remains the same: give to others the way Christ has given to us.

7. Making Disciples. At the core of Jesus' Great Commission in Matthew 28:19–20 mentioned earlier is the direct command to "go." It was never God's design for the church to remain idle or comfortable in one place. We are called by our Leader to branch out, share our testimonies, love others, build relationships, and eventually share the life-changing, soul-saving gospel of Jesus! It isn't enough just to do good things for others; we must deliberately and intentionally tell people about Christ and how we are to give our lives to him in order to be saved!

The fundamental reason I took the time to write this book was to get us back to, well, the fundamentals of our faith. I believe with all my heart that the church is experiencing the pains it's experiencing because we have continued to build the church without the fundamentals being securely put in place. Without the firm foundation of what the Bible has called us to do, we will ultimately not succeed in the things that truly matter to God. The heart of Jesus is for his church to make disciples, baptize, and teach. If we are to create a culture that is both welcoming and not compromising of the fundamentals of the faith and the Bible, we must first know what those fundamental roles of the church are according to his Word.

So I have provided for you what these fundamentals are to our community. Do you agree with these fundamentals? Are there some that you may not see as key to the faith, or maybe something that you feel like I have omitted that is near to your heart? The key is asking what God thinks and going back to his Word for the answers.

TAKE AN INVENTORY:

1. What are your thoughts on the majors listed in this chapter? Would you add or take away any of them?
2. What dangers arise when churches don't make their majors and minors clear? Have you personally seen divisions based on these things?

CHAPTER 11

THE CHURCH MUST PURSUE AN EXCELLENCE WHICH HONORS GOD AND OTHERS.

"We don't strive for excellence to boast on ourselves; we strive for excellence to boast on a most excellent God. At the end of the day, this is our offering. So just as one would give their best at their career or education, why wouldn't we also give that diligence plus more to the Creator of the Universe?"

—Kyle Elkins, former Air Traffic Controller, now Worship Pastor at The Experience Community

If we are going to create a personal culture that leads to a church culture that makes disciple-making disciples, we must do everything to the best of our abilities. Ecclesiastes 9:10 is a pivotal Scripture in my personal life and in our church. Solomon simply tells us that we are to do the best we can at whatever we put our hands on. I often tell my very intelligent daughters that I am completely content with them getting a C in a class as long as that was their best effort. I tell them, "We don't expect A's; we expect your best."

From the local church, however, we should expect our very best, *and* our very best should never be C-level. We may not have the ability to do everything, but whatever we choose to do, we had better do it 100 percent in order to honor God and reach the people around us. Whenever the church is sloppy (I almost used a reference to half of a donkey), the people coming into our services recognize it. The secular world is constantly trying to be more efficient, cleaner, faster, and sharper. If the world is trying so hard to be excellent, I think the church should do an even better job.

We take tremendous care with things that most people may find insignificant. Announcements, for example, and how we communicate events at our church are done with meticulous efficiency. In fact, overcommunication is one of our team's core values, and it is plastered ten feet wide on our office wall. We understand at The Experience Community that communicating to thousands of people over three campuses is challenging and extremely important. If one of our team members needs to get a meeting or event announced, they must go through several months of planning and designing through our creative team. They must reach a point of clarity on the event for whoever will be doing the announcements that week. They have to work with social media, the website, and the app schedule to make sure other events or announcements don't get drowned out in the process. I know that to many that sounds not only cumbersome but maybe even a bit extreme. To our team, however, we see it as being diligent and excellent for the sake of announcing and communicating important steps that lead people into the next stage of their growth in Jesus at our church.

We also take great care with cleanliness and things being in order. There have been several articles and studies that have shown that some of the biggest reasons families don't return to a church are the dirty bathrooms or the chaotic nursery and children's area. What a terrible reason to miss an opportunity for new families to get connected into the local church! Though it may seem a little maniacal to some, we do frequent walkabouts, hold our teams accountable for the order and cleanliness of their environments, and diligently make sure every corner of our building is orderly and clean.

People can often confuse excellence with extravagance, but they are not the same thing. I don't believe the church should ever be known for all-you-can-eat, buffet-style extravagance, but that we should always pursue excellence. In fact, I think it was God's design that The Experience Community could never afford to be extravagant. All throughout our first ten years of being a church, we never had much money. Though we have caught up over time, our lack of financial resources pushed us to be creative with the things we did have. Where we lacked in wealth, we made up in creativity and excellence. Though we looked like a scrappy group of young Christians, we did everything with extreme precision and care. Our team caught the vision that if corporate America and the entertainment industry do everything they can to be excellent and precise, the church should exceed that because we have a higher purpose than the marketplace or entertainment industry.

We may not always have much as far as material resources are concerned, but with what we do have, we should honor God to the best of our abilities. This not only honors God; it shows that we love the people that sacrifice their time to experience our church. And when we don't have much as far as material resources, we have still been given much by God to steward. We have been given the only message that will save and change mankind. We have been given the commission of going out and teaching, baptizing, and making disciples of people from our neighborhoods in middle Tennessee to the remotest islands in Lake Victoria, Africa. God never promised earthly resources, but he did promise power and the help of the Holy Spirit, and with these things much is expected from us.

Excellence is at the core of what we do because the Author of excellence has called us to do it and has given us the tools necessary for being the brightest light in our communities! We are called to do things well because we honor the Great One.

When we show this level of care and when we are willing to be held accountable for how well we do things in our personal lives and in the church, we will be putting another piece of the puzzle into place.

TAKE AN INVENTORY:

1. Can you honestly say that you give the work of the ministry your best?
2. What are practical and simple things you and your local church can do to be excellent in everything you do?

PART 3

HOW DO WE SEND DISCIPLES OUT TO REPLICATE THE PROCESS?

This portion of the book is mostly designed for the leaders in a church that have input into the direction, or at least the implementation, of the local church. Again, I know not everyone who picks this book up has the authority or voice to make all the changes necessary in their church, but at the very least this next section can be a spark that ignites some conversation amongst Christians that have a desire to see people become empowered disciples that go out into their communities or surroundings and make more disciples of Jesus Christ.

This third section is something of a 30,000-foot view of how we at The Experience have begun the process of multiplication and empowerment of disciples and leaders. We have not figured it all out or "arrived." We are constantly evolving and evaluating our processes, but one thing remains the same: we do everything in order to be as efficient and aggressive as possible with fulfilling the Great Commission.

CHAPTER 12

EMPOWER PEOPLE TO GO OUT AND FISH.

I will go ahead and be the jerk that claims that many people can grow a church while also not fulfilling the most important of all post-resurrection commands from Jesus: make disciples. In our current Christian culture, we have followed the world's lead by creating a cult of personality when it comes to pastors and church leaders. In many cases, the attractive and charismatic performer (we often call them pastors) is the sole reason for the large attendance. They look good, they encourage us, they never ask us to sacrifice (unless it's money to their ministry), and they don't give us too much Bible, just the Scripture that lifts us up. Best of all, we will be "blessed" without having to experience any disruption to our lifestyles.

I know every generation has their share of "itching ears," but through our extremely easy and fast methods via social media, we can create personality idols almost overnight. What is absolutely remarkable about the expansive followings of such popular leaders is that the church in the United States continues to shrink in biblical literacy and true discipleship. Even our numbers of people going to church services continues to decline overall despite our desperate efforts to court this generation into identifying as Christian.

As I have said several times throughout this book, we have many churches call or come by to get consultation on how we do things. The main goal for most churches is growth. It isn't that the hearts of these pastors are evil, but for some reason most church leaders have been led to believe that growth is the only marker of an effective church. Let me be clear: I don't think growth is unimportant. I get frustrated when people say it's not about numbers. Well, of course it is! We want more people to go to heaven than burn in eternal hell. However, the problem is not simply growing, but *how* we are growing (or not growing). I think if churches would focus on the Great Commission in its entirety, the church would naturally grow. That means that in order for the church to grow well, we must make authentic disciples of Jesus.

Let's circle back to all the churches that contact us. I have found that they rarely if ever ask about the one thing that we put the most time, money, and energy into: discipleship. We must not only have a clear path for making mature followers of God, but we must equip them to go out and make more devoted followers of God. If we are not doing this, we are not being what Jesus himself told us to be.

Why do so many people shy away from true discipleship? I think it's because true discipleship is *tough*! It isn't something people can just throw money at or call in some keynote speaker to fix the problem overnight. Discipleship is getting into the mud with people. It opens us up to get hurt. It takes time and energy, and we will not always see immediate fruit. Discipleship is hard!

So how do we ensure that people are not only becoming followers of Christ but also fulfilling his mission to send out followers that make more followers? We have already laid the foundation for being authentic and intentional with our personal culture in order to invite people into the church. Once they come to church, we have discussed in great detail that the culture of the church must be both welcoming and biblically sound. Now, we must explore how we empower people to move from becoming a follower to going out and becoming "fishers of men" as Christ instructed us to be. This is not easily done and takes both tremendous prayer and strategy.

TAKE AN INVENTORY:

1. In your opinion, what keeps churches from empowering people to go out and make disciples?
2. Do you feel empowered to go out and make disciples? Why or why not?

CHAPTER 13

CREATE CLEAR EXPECTATIONS FOR EVERY STEP OF GROWTH IN THE CHURCH.

Let's return to one of our previous markers for a healthy church culture: clarity. If we are not clear about the road people need to travel, they will never reach the destination they need to reach. We have learned in the last eleven years that the hardest part of moving people through the discipleship process is the handoff between stages of growth. This is why it's so important that one of our team core values at The Experience is overcommunication. We have found that constant and clear communication about what is next is paramount in moving people closer to God and preparing them to be sent out into their world to "fish for men." Churches are usually pretty good about coming up with programs, events, and even good theological classes, but when it comes to a clear path of growth and clear path of releasing them out into their worlds, churches fail most of the time.

In order to be clear, we must also be simple. This doesn't mean we can't do excellent or even complex things, but we must make the process of completing the step and getting to the next extremely clear and simple. We must do everything we can to communicate with simplicity the process of discipleship and empowering to disciple.

Process of Discipleship

The above diagram shows the simple steps we want people in our churches to go through. The process is deliberately designed to be extremely simple.

1. Worship. This involves making weekend services a priority. Hebrews 10:25 tells us that the gathering of Christians, which is for the sake of worship, hearing the word, and communion, is vitally important in the life of the believer and should continue until Jesus returns. This first step is the one that every person, regardless of past and even present sins, is welcome to be a part of. People often ask about church discipline, but we believe the weekend services and worship events are the wide-open door for anyone to visit and see what we are about.

2. Next Class. This is where we give newcomers a tour of the facilities, share the testimony of the pastor, and tell them the history of the church. We encourage people to ask questions fielded by members of our team that represent various steps in our process. This night is one of our most effective ways to get people into the next steps of our church. We have about 150–200 people a month come through this two-and-a-half-hour class and tour. We are relentless about announcing these classes, and we absolutely never miss a month. At the end of this class, we try to urge people into our "Following Jesus" course, which in turn puts them into the next three steps of our discipleship process.

3. Community. This is our network of small groups (which we call Life Groups). We talk about these on our app and website, and we even have a kiosk station in our sanctuary that tells people about all of the groups which are still open. We push groups as adamantly as we can because it is in these groups, not in our weekend services, where people find pastoral care and connection with others. Though our church is large, people can still easily get lost in a church one-twentieth of our size. Regardless of the size of church, we need each other. Small groups are the best way we have found to have accountability and community.

4. Development. These are classes designed to take people deeper into their faith. As mentioned earlier, we begin with "Following Jesus," a seven-week class that leads new believers (and even many longtime Christians who don't know the basics of the Christian faith) through the basics of Christianity. We cover prayer and worship, the importance of the Bible, baptism and communion, the Trinity, the church, and sharing your faith and the Great Commission. From there we move them into "Authentic Discipleship," which uses Jim

Putnam's *Real-Life Discipleship* workbook. We also offer what we call "electives"—for example, Financial Peace University, GriefShare, DivorceCare, and Celebrate Recovery.

5. Serving. The last stage that we hope everyone will reach is serving, either inside or outside of our church. We are constantly making people aware through our Vision Services and weekly announcements of opportunities to serve. We also communicate the need to help with the nonprofits we support in our community.

This process is not always linear, but the steps are clear as to where we want our congregation to go. In fact, the process would be more accurately shown as circular in nature (see the diagram below). There will be times that people are involved in serving before they get into a small group, or they may attend some of our development classes before they make it to a Next Class. The point is a progressive movement towards Christ.

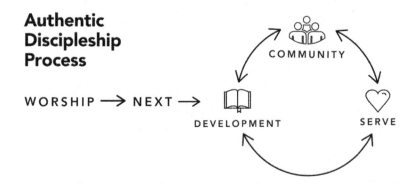

Authentic Discipleship Process

WORSHIP → NEXT → DEVELOPMENT → COMMUNITY → SERVE

As the above diagram shows in a more circular manner, we want to move new believers through a simple process that both educates them and holds them accountable as they grow deeper in their relationship with Christ. It may look easy on paper, but communicating to a large group of people the seemingly simple process of becoming disciples and then disciple-makers can be pretty frustrating and take a lot of strategy. This is probably why most churches don't have a clear discipleship path. There are two important, overarching things we are looking for to gauge if people are moving through our process:

1. Baptism. Baptizing people is not only commanded by Christ in the Great Commission, it is also the clearest way to gauge if the church is at least in the beginning stages of making disciples.

2. Moving People into an Active Position in the Church. This can be serving, moving into deeper development classes (GriefShare, DivorceCare, Financial Peace, or any of the other classes we may be offering), or putting them into a Life Group.

Levels of Involvement

We have tiers of service involvement at The Experience Community. Each level of involvement requires a deeper commitment and responsibility. As we get people plugged into the various areas of the church, we want them to understand that discipleship requires maturation and integrity. I feel like too many churches are way too lax in their standard for how people can serve. I also believe that we are doing people a huge disservice by not informing and equipping them to take a step up. These are our levels of involvement:

Level 1. This is someone who regularly attends church and has gone to Next Class. At this first level, we allow anyone who comes to church and has gone to "Next" to serve. These are service opportunities like hospitality, parking, and possibly the production booth. These are places where people struggling with virtually anything can get involved and start their walk with the church family.

Level 2. In addition to regular attendance and completion of Next, this person has been baptized (not necessarily in our church) and has signed up for or been through "Following Jesus." Positions in this level include serving in children's areas, student areas, and the production booth, as well as anything in Level 1.

Level 3. In addition to meeting the previous expectations, this person is in a small group and has been told of the expectation of tithing. This level consists of more leadership roles. The leadership role we focus on most at this level is leadership in small groups and on the stage, for example, in our worship team. We consider our small group leaders to be the deacon roles of our church, so the accountability of Level 3 is very important to us.

Level 4. In addition to all of the previous requirements, at this level we also check faithful tithing. This is the highest level of involvement. When people are on this level, they are in a position to be hired or become elders in our church. We believe in tithing and teach it to our entire church, but at this level we actually check on tithing because these will potentially be people that will make financial decisions at our church.

Though all of this looks fairly simple from the surface, the implementation and communication of this process is extremely difficult and must be tweaked and focused on virtually all the time. Discipleship and equipping the saints to go out and tell others about Christ are two of the most important things the church is responsible for. We firmly believe that how we implement our processes is constantly, and should be constantly, evolving and growing.

In the most practical way, let me share with you how easy this looks on paper, but how difficult it can be in real-life situations. We have a large number of gay and lesbian individuals that attend our weekend service, and recently we have been having more transgendered people as well. The Level 1 involvement is open to all people, including the LGBT community. The difficult thing about this is that the LGBT lifestyle is out in the open most of the time, and transgenderism is blatantly out in the open. What I mean is that their sin is visible whereas most others are hidden. So though it may make some people uncomfortable, and though we may have to take it on a case-by-case basis, we let these people serve on a safe level. If we discriminate and make one sin higher than another (after all, sex before marriage is a much bigger problem in our churches than same-sex relationships), we will never reach a community that already feels ostracized by Christians.

I want to encourage you to ask if your church has a clear path to take believers on in order to make them more fully devoted disciples and disciple-makers of Jesus. If we fail to create a clear path and target, we cannot be frustrated when the people in our churches have no idea where to go and how to get there. Solomon in all of his wisdom made it clear: "Where there is no vision, the people perish"

(Prov. 29:18, KJV). If we do the hard work of creating a clear path of discipleship, we can start to identify leaders in our churches that may have the potential to go out and make more disciples and even plant and pastor churches.

TAKE AN INVENTORY:

1. Does your church have a discipleship process? Is the discipleship process of your church clear and simple? How is it communicated (or not communicated)?
2. Are the expectations of people being discipled and serving in your church clear? What can you do to make the process clearer?

CHAPTER 14

EQUIP THE NEXT GENERATION OF LEADERS.

We seem to have a hard time sending people out from our churches, but let's not forget that releasing leaders to go for the sake of greater ministry was commanded and modeled by Jesus. Also, many church leaders have a very difficult time letting others lead in the first place, mainly because there is a fear that our numbers may not look as big or someone else may outshine us and take some of our thunder. Remember, we are being honest here.

I remember the first time I let our Experience Community Cannon County Pastor, Josh Brooker, teach. Josh has a master's degree in a subject that I only hold an undergraduate degree in (English), and he is an extremely educated and gifted speaker. For weeks I had people telling me how much they loved hearing him teach, and one lady had even told him that if he left to start another church, she would instantly go with him. Okay, in the spirit of transparency, it was a bit of a blow to my ego. For the first time, I had a younger, more educated, and very gifted communicator step into my pulpit and teach just as well if not better than I ever had. This could have been seen as the prime time to limit and even shut down such a potential threat to one's power, but I didn't see it like that. I trusted that God was blessing me with a more talented leader than I and that it is the heart of God to let the ones after us do even greater things than what we have done.

Over the years, I not only let Josh teach more and more, I officially made him the next in line for my job. I would joke that if a truck hit me, Josh is the man. When we started our second campus, I asked Josh to be the lead pastor there. As of today, Josh has almost 500 people in a town that is only 2,000 people in total. He has moved out to Woodbury, Tennessee, and become one of the most influential people in his community. Now Josh is preparing people to go out from his church to plant even further out in rural areas around Tennessee.

We often think that letting others lead will somehow diminish our importance, but what it actually does is make us look like even better leaders. Even if we were thinking completely selfishly, we should still recognize this truth. For example, let's theoretically take out the biblical principle that we are to follow in the footsteps of Christ and develop leaders that go to greater lengths than we did. Let's take out the Great Commission and take out the model of Paul and Timothy. Even from a worldly leadership perspective, creating great leaders will make the first leader look better! I think that if I could just convince some pastors about this very worldly benefit of creating leaders, I could get some control freaks to do some more efficient and expansive work for the kingdom of God!

So let me tell you where The Experience Community is right now in developing and sending out high-level leadership. We do a two-year program that takes men and women in whom we see potential and walks them through one year of theology, leadership training, and teaching skills. Then, in the second year, we hire on all the cohort as interns. They get to see the inner workings of the church and to shadow me and others on my team. The hope is that after these two years, we now have at least four teams of people that can go out and start churches with a similar DNA to The Experience Community.

Our hope is to create a strong personal culture in the men and women we are sending out. If they have a good personal culture, and they have been discipled in a good church culture, they will not only lead healthy and growing churches, they will make more disciples that make disciples. More disciples of Jesus is not only the pinnacle of success for our church; it is the heart of Jesus himself.

TAKE AN INVENTORY:

1. If you are being brutally honest, why is it so hard for you to let others flourish and succeed?
2. Do you have a plan to develop leaders and plant more churches? If not, why?

CHAPTER 15

EMPOWER DISCIPLES OF JESUS TO MAKE MORE DISCIPLES.

Explaining disciple-making is both simple and complex. I think the main goal of a church should be first to create a culture of people who are building relationships with other people that honor God by bringing others closer to him. Throughout this book, I have tried to show how I build relationships (although I am still in the works) and how our church moves people through development. No matter how many people you disciple, discipleship remains an ongoing, lifelong process that never rests and is ever evolving in our complex and confused world. Yet the heart of discipleship never changes. We want to make followers of Christ that long to make more followers of Christ.

To go back to the beginning of this book for a moment, perhaps we need to rethink discipleship. Instead of thinking of evangelism and discipleship as different processes, maybe we should view our first conversation when starting a relationship as the beginning of discipleship, even if that relationship is with a nonbeliever. Does that mean that nonbelievers can be disciples? Well, yes and no. I think the more fundamental question is whether discipleship begins before a person completely converts. I think the answer to this is *yes*. Jesus called fishermen and began discipling them before they fully understood what was happening or who he was. Maybe the first interactions with people are actually the beginning of the discipleship process.

So how do we empower our people to personally make disciples? We first challenge them to view all people as individuals made in the image of God. All people? Yes! The gay couple, the Muslim, the atheist, and the lukewarm nominal Christian are all people that we should engage and build a relationship with in order to hopefully lead them to Christ. We must create a culture in our church that diligently teaches and lives a lifestyle insulated by the Holy Spirit, not isolated from a hurting world. What fear does the light have in darkness? None. Light always overcomes darkness.

Once a relationship forms, what do we do next? I think the macro idea of discipleship contains the following key elements:

1. **Communication.** This means talking with each other and doing life together. We must get to know people that we are walking with. This involves going to coffee on a weekly basis, meeting in a small group, getting lunch, or even doing FaceTime together.
2. **Accountability.** Discipling relationships are willing to hear and speak hard truths. This includes the ability and willingness to let "iron sharpen iron." This means we ask hard questions and commit to giving hard answers. Without brutal honesty and accountability, discipleship is impossible.
3. **Teaching.** Without the Word and sound theology, there is no disciple of Jesus. We must not only be grounded in

the Word, but we must also teach others the importance of biblical integrity.

4. **Listening.** We must learn to listen and empathize. The more I pastor, the more I realize most people just need someone to whom they can confess and vent their feelings. Sometimes we need to talk less and listen more.

5. **Equipping.** We must not only teach them biblical truths but also train them to do the work of the ministry and lead others. This equipping may come via many different resources, but, whatever the method, it must be intentional. It can mean reading books together, going through some kind of curriculum, or listening to a podcast and discussing it.

6. **Releasing.** We must eventually multiply and release others to go be disciple-makers. This is the Jesus model.

The previous list gives simple steps for one-on-one discipleship. How those steps play out may look different for every relationship. This is because culture and social settings can vary drastically, not only around the world but within the United States itself.

I think a valuable point to remember is to be dedicated to the process while not overcomplicating it. This means we must consistently talk, meet, hold each other accountable, learn, and equip—but stay fluid enough to allow for mistakes and setbacks. We are not perfect people, but we lean on a perfect God to show us grace when we need help. We must not remove the Spirit from our work as disciples. If we are connected to him, we will allow him to lead and guide us.

TAKE AN INVENTORY:

1. By this time in the book, you have heard the word *process* quite a bit. Has the importance of process started to sink in? Are you thinking of simple and reproducible ways to make more disciples and leaders?

YOU ARE NOT JESUS.

Memorial Day 2018 may have been the worst day I have ever experienced while doing ministry. That morning I had reached out to a young husband who had been unfaithful to his wife. Several weeks before I reached out, he had sent disturbing, cryptic emails and texts to some people on my staff but would never tell us who he was, making it impossible for us to reach back out to him. Well, we did some research and found out who had been sending us the anonymous messages, so I took about thirty minutes on Memorial Day morning to call him and try to set up a time for us to meet later that week. This young man was someone that his wife and I had been trying to get involved in the church for years, but to no avail. He never showed any interest in committing to church, and he refused to turn from his addictions and reckless lifestyle.

The young man kept insisting that I come over immediately, but I told him that I had plans with my family. I could do any other time that week, but not on Memorial Day because I already had plans to be with my wife, my kids, and my best friend's family at their house. He said he understood, and that we would meet later that week and talk. Immediately after that phone call, I called the man's wife and advised her to not communicate with her husband in person, but to let me talk to him this week and then we could work on getting to the root of their issues.

The day went on. We ate with our friends and their families, played in the yard, and went home to relax. I was out cleaning my car when I got a phone call from Kyle, our worship leader. He shakily told me that the husband had gone over to see the wife, shot her, her dad, and her stepmother, and then turned the gun on himself. I remember tracing back every step our church and I took leading up to this tragic event. I asked myself if we had covered every base, asked every question, and taken every opportunity to do what was right and fix this broken man who ended up committing a triple homicide and suicide. With all honesty and humility, I can answer before God and man and say I and our church did everything we could to help this man before he chose to do what he did.

Even in the most extreme circumstances, we have to trust and believe that the only true Savior of mankind is Jesus Christ, and all we can do is our best to build the bridge for more people to know him. With virtually every person I try to counsel and connect with, there is always a sense of "I am this person's only hope." Not only is this idea the pinnacle of arrogance, but it is also a lie from Satan.

The most challenging thing for me since I have started doing ministry is that I cannot control the results of what I do. I am a fixer by nature, and when I can't see immediate results, or even long-term results, I get frustrated and easily discouraged. Yet Jesus never told us that we are responsible for the salvation of others. Nor do the Gospels or epistles of the

New Testament tell us that when we do all the prep work and follow the instruction from God correctly that everyone will convert and follow Christ. We are simply called to plant and water. We are called to cultivate environments in which God can move in people's hearts and save their souls. For fixers like myself, this is a hard truth to grapple with.

I remember one of my sessions with my wonderful counselor when he scolded me for constantly talking about my failure to hold onto all the people I have poured into over the years. I was in the middle of a vicious attack from several people for whom our church and I specifically had done a lot. The situation got so bad that I had to involve lawyers and issue a cease-and-desist order against one of the more verbal critics of our church. I told my counselor how heartbreaking it can be that the ones we seem to do the most for are the ones that can turn around and hurt us the most. I sat there and went through everything I could have possibly done better and why I didn't do this or why I did do what I did when John interrupted me.

He asked me, "Corey, are you Jesus? Are you the only Jesus these people have been exposed to?" I remember just kind of sitting there stunned. Well, of course I am not Jesus, but subconsciously I was trying to be the savior.

His point was that we are not the fixers of humanity. We are instruments of the Master, and only he is capable of fixing people. This doesn't mean that we do not have a level of responsibility. It doesn't mean that we are not called to be salt and light of the world. But it does mean that, regardless of how well we create a personal and church culture of making disciples, not everyone will respond in the way we would hope.

I firmly believe God has given us the task of preparing, strategizing, and "calculating the cost" before building something (Luke 14:28). I think we honor God when we put everything we have into the work of the ministry and to loving, communicating with, and reaching out to hurting people around us. Yet, even at our best and even with God's hand deep into what we are doing, some people simply will not receive the truth. There is great liberation in 1 Corinthians 3:6: "I planted, Apollos watered, but God gave the growth." This simple passage shows us that we are responsible to cultivate conversations, show grace and love, be excellent at what we do, and hold onto the truth we know. Yet, although we do those things, it is *God* that makes things happen.

I am learning that it all goes back to a deep dependency on him. I know that we are saved by grace through faith, I know that my works are filthy rags compared to the Savior's, and I know that I am utterly lost without God's help and guidance. Though books like this may be able to help us look at the "what" and the "how" when we are reaching out to the world, at the end of the day all glory and credit goes to God. Maybe the biggest folly of pastors, vocational ministers, lay leaders, and congregants is that we don't live in more dependence on Christ and his work on the cross. We tend to "lean on our own understanding" more than we depend on the Word and the spiritual gifts of wisdom, knowledge, and discernment.

I hope this book has been a blessing and a tool amongst many that you use to help reach the lost for Jesus Christ. Even more than that, I hope that we all can find more solace in him. The only personal and church culture that will ever save the souls of mankind and change our schools, neighborhoods, families, and relationships is a culture centered on God and his principles. If we can lean more into him, be mindful of how we interact with others, and build a church experience that is authentic and has biblical integrity, we can see amazing things happen in our communities!

Though it is a passage we may have heard a thousand times, we must remember the vitally important words of our Savior: "You will have suffering in this world. Be courageous! I have conquered the world" (John 16:33). Be encouraged and empowered by the Holy Spirit!

ENDNOTES

1. "Culture Wheel," *NMAC*, August 6, 2019 http://www.nmac.org/culture-usca-whats-happening-in-2019/culture-wheel/ (accessed July 15, 2020).

2. David Kinnaman and Mark Matlock, *Faith for Exiles: 5 Ways for a New Generation to Follow Jesus in Digital Babylon* (Grand Rapids: Baker, 2019), 33.

3. Bobby Harrington, "Top Trends in Disciple Making in 2020," *Discipleship.org* https://discipleship.org/bobbys-blog/disciple-making-trends-2020/ (accessed July 15, 2020).

4. "National Study on Disciple Making in USA Churches: High Aspirations Amidst Disappointing Results," *discipleship.org*, 2020, https://discipleship.org/national-study-on-disciple-making-in-usa-churches/ (accessed July 15, 2020).

5. John F. Kennedy, "Ask Not What Your Country Can Do for You," *US History* https://www.ushistory.org/documents/ask-not.htm.

6. Tom S. Rainer and Eric Geiger, *Simple Church: Returning to God's Process for Making Disciples* (Nashville: B&H Publishing Group, 2011).

7. Jim Putman, *Real-Life Discipleship: Building Churches That Make Disciples* (Colorado Springs: NavPress, 2010).

ABOUT THE AUTHOR

COREY TRIMBLE became a believer in 2002 after living a life of addiction and playing music for several years on the road with multiple punk/hardcore bands. He graduated with a BA in English Literature from Middle Tennessee State University and went on to teach high school and college English. Although Corey has never attended formal seminary, he became a student pastor in 2005 before leaving the church where he became a Christian to start The Experience Community in 2009. Corey is very open about his shortcomings and insecurities, which makes his pastoring style unique and refreshing.

Made in the USA
Monee, IL
17 December 2020